Bigger Barns

Living Content in a Material World

Pam Gillaspie

Acknowledgements

Thanks so much to the classes who have graciously piloted this class with me both in person and online. Your feedback and encouragement have spurred me on. Thank you to my hubby, Dave, for your design and layout and to my girls, Jackie and Katie, for your input on style and design. Thanks to Mary Ann Lamb and Shelly Stansfield for your help in copy-editing and proofreading. Finally, a big thank you to Dr. Mike Vanlangham for providing theological editing to make sure I'm on the straight and narrow.

Unless otherwise specified, Scriptures
are taken from the NEW AMERICAN STANDARD BIBLE®,
© Copyright 1960, 1962, 1963, 1968, 1971, 1972, 1973, 1975, 1977, 1995 by The Lockman Foundation.
Used by permission. (www.Lockman.org)

Scripture marked NKJV taken from the New King James Version®. Copyright © 1982 by Thomas Nelson. Used by permission. All rights reserved.

Bigger Barns: Living Content in a Material World

Copyright © 2024 by Pam Gillaspie
Published by IGNITE Bible Ministries

ISBN: 978-0-9978503-3-8

All rights reserved. No part of this book may be reproduced, translated, or transmitted in any form or by any means, electronic or mechanical, including photocopying, recording, or by any information storage and retrieval system, without permission in writing from the publisher.

Printed in the United States of America

2024

TABLE OF CONTENTS

INTRODUCTION: **WRITING TO MYSELF** 4

LESSON ONE: **I'LL BUILD A BIGGER BARN** 7

LESSON TWO: **THE BEAUTY OF LESS.** 21

LESSON THREE: **EXTRACTING THE PRECIOUS** 39

LESSON FOUR: **DISORDER AND EVERY EVIL THING** .. 57

LESSON FIVE: **QUESTIONS TO ASK MYSELF** 69

LESSON SIX: **FOR WHAT PURPOSE?** 85

About the Study

Every lesson has two components designed to encourage you to dig deeper while also exploring Scripture more widely. Each will complement without being dependent on the other.

You'll interact with a few short Scripture passages and answer some questions about the text.

You'll find suggested books of the Bible to listen to while you work your way though some daily decluttering.

Resources

In this workbook you will have an opportunity to use additional study tools. Here are some of our favorites which are available as websites or mobile apps. We are grateful for these ministries that provide excellent and accessible Bible study resources for all.

www.biblehub.com   Bible Hub is a production of the Online Parallel Bible Project. This project is privately owned and supported for the express purpose of sharing Bible study tools online.

www.blueletterbible.com   Blue Letter Bible provides powerful tools for an in-depth study of God's Word through their free online reference library, with study tools that are grounded in the historical, conservative Christian faith.

www.biblegateway.com   Bible Gateway is a searchable online Bible in more than 200 versions and 70 languages that you can freely read, research, and reference anywhere. With a library of audio Bibles, a mobile app, devotionals, email newsletters, and other free resources, Bible Gateway equips you not only to read the Bible, but to understand it.

INTRODUCTION

Writing to Myself

Welcome To My Mess!

From time to time people ask me, "How do you decide what to write about?" It's a good question, I think. Here are both the concise and not-so-concise answers. The concise answer is: I write what I believe God is prompting me to write about. Simple. God prompts and I respond in obedience to the best of my ability.

The long answer, though, is more nuanced. Sometimes my heart is burdened for hurts and problems I see in the people around me. My first Bible study, *Sweeter than Chocolate! Psalm 119* came from a broken heart as I looked around and realized so many people inside the church walls viewed the Bible as a "have to." To them, reading the Bible was the spiritual equivalent of eating their vegetables.

My heart broke over people missing the joy and the sweetness of God's Word, and my prayer became "LORD! How do I help people understand that Your Word is sweet, that it is more like chocolate than broccoli?" I never heard an audible voice or saw handwriting on a wall, but He answered by continuing to bring me to Psalm 119:103: "How sweet are Your words to my taste, yes, sweeter than honey to my mouth." Before I had time to second guess and talk myself out of it, I immersed myself in studying and writing about Psalm 119 with the hope of helping others experience the sweetness of God's Word for themselves.

> ***"Yes, this is a study but it is also a journal of my journey of throwing off encumbrances to live as nimbly as possible for Christ and His Kingdom."***

Other times I write in response to concerns I have for the church corporate. The prevalence of what is sometimes called a "soft gospel"—that is the "gospel" proclaimed not as the power of God, but as the cherry on top of an already good life—permeating many quarters of the visible church prompted me to write *Solid Truth for Slippery Times* an inductive Bible study on Galatians. Paul's corrective letter to the Galatians shows a church in danger of falling away from the true Gospel.

Still other times, I write what I need. I often hear from people who have benefited from the study *No Worries* that I co-authored with Jan Silvious. I'm glad God has used this study in others' lives, but the truth is I wrote that book for me. Worry has been a formidable opponent in my life. In many ways it has been a double-agent pretending to be on my side, promising to make me smarter, to know more, to pay attention better. Yeah, my worry promised to make me like God! Alas, we all know how that lie pans out.

So why all this talk about why I write? Well, here's the thing, **Bigger Barns** is another study that I need for me . . . but I'm guessing I'm not alone. Sure there are a million and one books that can and will tell you how to deal with your stuff—and you will probably want to grab one of the those or dust off one that you already have in a pile somewhere to help with the nuts and bolts—but most of these stop short of dealing with the spiritual components of stuff from a biblical worldview. I need the power of truth and the power of the Holy Spirit in order to work through my stuff, both literally and figuratively.

So as we move forward, know that I am writing first and foremost to myself. If something sounds unduly harsh, know that you are the secondary audience. Yes, this is a study but it is also a journal of my journey of throwing off encumbrances to live as nimbly as possible for Christ and His Kingdom.

If I haven't scared you away yet, let's get started.

LESSON ONE

I'll Build a Bigger Barn

BIGGER AND BETTER, NEW AND IMPROVED

As I write this book, my husband and I are living in the third residence of our married lifetime. We spent our first three years in a tiny one-bedroom apartment so small that we had to remove the bedroom door in order for our bed to fit in the room. Our sole television was a 13-inch beauty with a built-in VHS player and the most amazing remote control that popped right into the front of the unit for safe keeping when not in use. Our big splurge, a portable dishwasher, rolled up to the kitchen faucet every time we ran it.

We had next to nothing (at least compared to now), but at the same time we lacked nothing and accumulated little. Okay, we accumulated some—every time a new *Far Side* book by Gary Larson released we'd splurge. We lived in college housing so we knew that world was not our home and that like it or not, when I graduated, we'd be on our way somewhere else. When you know you're not setting up shop permanently, you stay a bit more nimble.

We purchased our first house with a 7-year balloon payment, with the intent to move to a more child-friendly house within a few years. We stayed for about four and a half years but many of our purchases—the carpet and other home improvement items—stayed at the 3-bedroom Keith Avenue home.

Lesson One
I'll Build a Bigger Barn

The current place? It's four bedrooms with a full basement. We've been here over 25 years. Sigh. After 25 years, stuff piles up even if you're trying to keep the influx low. Stuff piles up, even when you develop regular rhythms of throwing things away—at least it does for mere mortals like my people and me.

Statistics say that the Gillaspies are not alone in having both too much space and too much stuff. Between the years 1973 and 2016, new homes in the United States have grown about 1,000 square feet bigger and the people living in those houses have almost twice as much room to knock around in as households (the people in the house) are shrinking as houses are growing. Instead of house sizes decreasing as the average number of people per house goes down, the United States continues to build bigger and bigger houses.

As a nation, we watch shows ranging from the lighthearted *Clean Sweep* (no longer on the air, but my all-time favorite decluttering show) to the more frightening *Hoarders* hoping to find a way to deal with our "treasures." Marie Kondo tells us to keep what "sparks joy" while Peter Walsh tells us to "lighten up" and "let it go." A quick Google search will give you more tips and strategies than you'll be able to absorb.

The problem remains. If we don't address the heart issues, the best we will find ourselves accomplishing is varying levels of behavior modification—likely over and over as we start and stop, succeed and relapse often over months and years and even decades.

So, Google your favorite organizer for the professional strategies and then come along with me on my journey as I work through my remaining piles of stuff considering what God's Word has to say about my excess and my "treasure." Wow, I wish the pen was pointed at you and not me! ;) This could be a long six weeks!

Unpacking the Bags

Before we jump into God's Word, let's spend some time unpacking our bags. Don't worry, my bags are pretty full so know that I'm not expecting you to empty yours to the bottom right away, because I'm sure not ready to do that yet. Still, we need to begin assessing what we've got, where we're starting, and some of our current thinking about our stuff.

Why specifically did this study appeal to you? Do you need the help or are you hoping to find fixes for someone else? Explain.

If you're the one feeling overwhelmed, do you know where your hang-ups are? (For instance, my biggest hang-up is throwing away "memories." A close runner-up is "I might need it someday" items or "I should give this to a specific person" items). If you haven't thought about this, no worries. If you have and you know, write it down.

Why do you want to unload? What has prompted this? Is it your choice or someone else's idea?

If you've tried to get rid of things before, how have past purging parties gone?

What do you hope will be different once you've completed this study?

Are you committed to finishing the course and doing the hard work of application and obedience to what you learn as you study God's Word? What, if any, concerns do you have about getting started?

As we continue to study together, we'll think and talk through more of our stuff—physical and otherwise—and hold both up to the Word of God!

Lesson One
I'll Build a Bigger Barn

A Place for His Treasure

As we consider what God's Word has to say to us, let's look to a story Jesus told a man who was eager to pocket his portion of the family inheritance and wanted Jesus to help him do it!

Scripture:

READ Luke 12:13-21 and mark every reference to *possessions* (*inheritance, crops,* etc.)

Luke 12:13-21

13 *Someone in the crowd said to Him, "Teacher, tell my brother to divide the* family *inheritance with me."*

14 *But He said to him, "Man, who appointed Me a judge or arbitrator over you?"*

15 *Then He said to them, "Beware, and be on your guard against every form of greed; for not even when one has an abundance does his life consist of his possessions."*

16 *And He told them a parable, saying, "The land of a rich man was very productive.*

17 *"And he began reasoning to himself, saying, 'What shall I do, since I have no place to store my crops?'*

18 *"Then he said, 'This is what I will do: I will tear down my barns and build larger ones, and there I will store all my grain and my goods.*

19 *'And I will say to my soul, "Soul, you have many goods laid up for many years to come; take your ease, eat, drink and be merry."'*

20 *"But God said to him, 'You fool! This very night your soul is required of you; and now who will own what you have prepared?'*

21 *"So is the man who stores up treasure for himself, and is not rich toward God."*

Reason through the Scriptures:

What is the setting of the conversation? Who is involved?

Living Content in a Material World

Lesson One
I'll Build a Bigger Barn

How does the conversation start? What do you think of this?

What do we know about the man based on the question? (Don't read a story into this, just observe what is there.) Is there anything you would expect from a man in a similar situation?

How does Jesus respond to the man?

What warning does Jesus give? Who does He warn and how does He deliver the warning?

Do you think you struggle with greed? Why/why not? Explain your answer.

Can greed co-exist with serving God? Consider Matthew 6:24 as you answer. Explain your reasoning and any implications.

What greater underlying issue(s) do you think greed reveals? Again, considering Matthew 6:24, what does it show about our relationship to God?

Now, let's take a minute and follow the money. Look back at where you marked references to "possessions." Summarize the parable Jesus told paying attention to the assets. What were they? Where did they come from? What was the man going to do because of them? Etc.

What did you observe about the man's relationship to his possessions? What do you think about it? Do you relate? If so, in what ways?

Who does the man "talk to" about his stuff?

Have you ever brought your "stuff" questions to God? Do you seek His direction in what to do with your abundance or how to address your needs? Why/why not? How has that gone?

Lesson One
I'll Build a Bigger Barn

Living Content in a Material World

I've been battling the "stuff" monster for years. Now that the kids are grown and the influx has slowed, I feel like there's finally a chance for me to win the war!

Two friends who have helped me greatly in this area are my sister-in-law, Debbie, and my friend Diane. Debbie's the person who knows how to keep the right things and throw away (or sell!) everything else. She works hard, she plays hard, and she knows how to squeeze blood out of a nickel. I'm sure if she happened to throw the wrong thing, she'd be able to reacquire an item of the same quality or better within three days at a third of the price. She has helped me purge the unnecessary while at the same time gifting our family *entirely helpful* items along the way such as furniture by being in the right place at the right time. She is an example in every way.

My friend, Diane, also lives simply and knows how to throw! In one "tossing" session years ago, she helped me learn to pray and ask God to help me know what needed to go. As odd as this may seem, praying about the situation is a great place to start. Too often, I'm like the man in Jesus' story who talks to himself. Maybe you are, too.

Instead of chatting with ourselves about our stuff, let's ask God to lead us through His Word into an understanding of true treasure and a proper relationship with the things of this life. Sidebar complete! Let's get back to the text . . .

What does the man think will happen? What is his goal, his intent for his life?

More specifically, who does he think is in control? How does that affect his behavior?

What actually happens?

How does God address the man? What question does He ask him?

While Jesus told a parable, what does He say the man in the story is like?

Even if we're not building bigger barns, what do *all* people have in common?

How should that affect our thinking, choices, and behavior?

Do you think of your material possessions with the really big picture in mind or is that too unsettling? Explain your answer.

Because we live in a broken and fallen world, everyone dies. Unless the Lord returns first, each one of us will die. You will, I will. As the old saying goes, "You can't take it with you, but you can send it ahead." Before we call it a day, let's take a look at Matthew's account of a similar teaching from Jesus.

Lesson One
I'll Build a Bigger Barn

The Place for Your Treasure

The disciple Matthew records one of Jesus' extended teachings in Matthew 5–7. It is often referred to as the Sermon on the Mount. Matthew tells us that Jesus taught these words to His disciples on a mountain in Galilee, an area located in the northern part of Israel.

Scripture:

READ Matthew 6:19-21 and mark every reference to *treasure(s)/store up* in the same way.

Matthew 6:19-21

19 *"Do not store up for yourselves treasures on earth, where moth and rust destroy, and where thieves break in and steal.*

20 *"But store up for yourselves treasures in heaven, where neither moth nor rust destroys, and where thieves do not break in or steal;*

21 *for where your treasure is, there your heart will be also.*

Reason through the Scriptures:

Use the chart below to compare what Jesus teaches about earthly versus heavenly treasure.

Earthly Treasure	Heavenly Treasure

How can you tell if something is merely earthly treasure?

Lesson One
I'll Build a Bigger Barn

What do you think Jesus has in mind when He refers to "treasures in heaven"? Explain from the text.

How is your treasure related to your heart?

Stuff on earth doesn't last although we like to think it will. Who of us hasn't bought the most durable or best quality at some point in hopes that it would "stand the test of time." Truth is, though, nothing does. Stuff does not have intrinsic value; it does not last.

Do you know what clarifies this principle for me more than anything else? Mouse poop. Yes, you read that right. Our house backs up on several acres of wooded property. When the snow begins flying in the winter, we're blessed by deer roaming on the outer edges of our yard . . . and we're cursed by the occasional mouse family who decides to shelter in our basement and snack in our kitchen. We've learned to set traps as the weather begins cooling, but the smart ones still take up residence from time to time.

You probably see where this is going. I can find myself locked up in a stay-or-go decision on a childhood treasure *until* I see mouse droppings in a box. The evidence of "mouse" clarifies my thinking. Mouse droppings? What I couldn't part with moments before, I can't get rid of quickly enough!

Earthly treasures can be stolen, they can rust, moths can eat them, floods can mold them, and mice can poop on them. This doesn't mean we need to burn the house down or that all temporal items are bad. You know that. The issue Jesus addresses is one of priority and focus.

Here or There?

So this week, as you consider the physical stuff in your house and items individually, ask yourself, *"Does this item incline my heart toward heaven or earth?"*

As you wade through your possessions, you will find that some of your items tie your heart and mind to your past or present and try to root you here, while others point you to God's faithfulness, kingdom truth, and your future in Jesus.

Let me explain one item from my past that points me forward. It is a picture of a relative that I never met, my great-grandmother Matilda Olson. On the back of the photograph my grandmother Margaret Olson recorded the following words:

> Mrs. Matilda Olson (nee Matilda Stam)
> Born in Onimskog - Dalsland, Sweden
> 1874 - passed away in 1954.
> Married Gottfrid Olson in Minneapolis, Minn. in 1903.
> He died in 1910.
> She was left with four boys - Roy, Harry, Walter and Donald. She raised them without Government help and kept them under the influence of the Lord Jesus Christ. Her efforts are marked by a line of Christian families.

Lesson One
I'll Build a Bigger Barn

This picture tells me part of my history and, more importantly, the history of my people with our God. Ultimately it points me to Jesus. It reminds me that when life is hard to fix my eyes on Jesus because God will not drop me. He was with my great-grandmother, with my grandfather, with my father, and is with me. This earthly object points my gaze towards Jesus and fixes my mind on His Kingdom.

Where to Start

If you have a favorite decluttering or organizational guru, look them up for their tips and strategies this week to get you started on the mechanics. Over the course of the next few weeks, you may want to hear input from different experts. Let's agree to work together room by room in the following order as we walk this path together. Start with 15 minutes a day assessing and purging and see how it goes. This week will be the kitchen and dining area.

Week 1—Kitchen / Dining

Week 2—Main Living Space—Living / Family Room

Week 3—Master Bedroom

Week 4—Other Bedrooms

Week 5—Office

Week 6—Bathrooms / Laundry

Before you jump into your kitchen, what are the two most important truths you learned this week from God's Word as it relates to your stuff? (I'm not fishing for a specific answer. I just want you to be clear on *your* two biggest application points.)

1.

2.

When you hit a wall this week, review your two key takeaways. If you've ever had trouble throwing things away, you will hit a wall. Let God's truth take you over, around, or through it.

Living Content in a Material World

Lesson One
I'll Build a Bigger Barn

WIDE

In the WIDE section of each lesson, we're going to listen to the Gospel accounts using your favorite audio Bible as we purge and consider how Jesus lived. Again, start with 15 minutes a day of listening and decluttering and see how it goes. Let's begin with the Gospel of Matthew as we start in the kitchen.

Each day, jot down something simple you'd like to remember from what you heard.

Day 1

Day 2

Day 3

Day 4

Day 5

Day 6

Day 7

YOUR BARN IS BIG ENOUGH!

Lesson One
I'll Build a Bigger Barn

LESSON TWO

The Desire for More, the Beauty of Less

WHERE DID IT ALL COME FROM?

My clutter journey has been a long one. I'm not buried in stuff by any means, but as much progress as I've made over the years, I still long to live a leaner, more streamlined life. Because of this, my ears are always opened to practical help and strategies from the experts. One of my favorite experts is Australian Peter Walsh formerly of TLC's *Clean Sweep*. In a recent podcast, Walsh, (a self-proclaimed non-religious person) addressed the helpfulness of what he calls "ancient wisdom literature," in this case the Old Testament of the Bible, in the battle against clutter. Can you guess where he went?

"You shall not covet . . ."
—Exodus 20:17

You may not feel like you have a coveting problem, but coveting or desiring more and more almost certainly played some role in landing both of us where we are today. Actions have consequences.

Until I heard Walsh address "You shall not covet," I was not heading to the Ten Commandments with this study. But his reference started me on the path of looking more closely at the word "covet" (Hebrew: *hamad*), and I can't wait to show you where it took me! Let's go!

Lesson Two
The Desire for More, the Beauty of Less

Bigger Barns

One of the Ten

To say that Peter Walsh shocked me when he connected clutter to a violation of one of the Ten Commandments is an understatement. A man who doesn't claim the God of the Bible and yet points to the wisdom of "You shall not covet" grabbed my attention. And so I headed off to look a little more closely at "You shall not covet," the detailed tenth of the Ten Commandments of Exodus 20. Let's look at it together.

Scripture:

The first five commandments of what is also referred to as the Decalogue concern man's relationship with God. The second grouping of five deal with people's relationships with one another. We'll focus our attention on the second five.

God gave the ten commandments to Moses on Mount Sinai after He delivered the people of Israel from slavery in Egypt.

READ Exodus 20:12-17 and mark references to *covet*. Underline everything the people are commanded not to covet.

> *Exodus 20:12-17*
>
> 12 "Honor your father and your mother, that your days may be prolonged in the land which the LORD your God gives you.
>
> 13 "You shall not murder.
>
> 14 "You shall not commit adultery.
>
> 15 "You shall not steal.
>
> 16 "You shall not bear false witness against your neighbor.
>
> 17 "You shall not covet your neighbor's house; you shall not covet your neighbor's wife or his male servant or his female servant or his ox or his donkey or anything that belongs to your neighbor."

While we're focusing on these six verses, you'll do well to read all of Exodus 20 for more context. While you can have too much clutter, you can never have too much context!

Reason through the Scriptures:

In the chart below, briefly list commandments five through ten and jot down who, in addition to God, is the offended party (if there is one) when a commandment is broken.

Commandment   **Offended Party (in Addition to God)**

5.

6.

7.

8.

9.

10.

As we observe the text of Scripture inductively, comparing and contrasting words and phrases in the text can help us notice elements we might typically overlook. For instance, commandment five differs in that it is a positive command ("Honor . . ."), while the next five are negative ("You shall not . . ."). How does the tenth commandment differ from the other five?

Is it easy to hide the sin of coveting from people? Explain.

Lesson Two
The Desire for More, the Beauty of Less

Bigger Barns

What does God tell the people not to covet? Do you see any connection between this commandment and any of the previous commandments? If so, which one(s) and how are they connected?

What do people covet today? Is there anything you covet?

Do you think *your* consumption ever sparks coveting in others? If so, why and how? One more before we leave this: Is this just "their" problem? Explain.

What role do you think social media plays in coveting and consumption today?

What kind of additional attitudes and behavior can coveting lead to?

How can coveting be tied to our clutter and material possessions?

The Beginning of Discontent

Before we move forward, we need to take a short step back to explore the word translated "covet" a bit more closely. The Hebrew word *hamad* enters the biblical scene well before the giving of the Law at Sinai. In fact, the first instance of *hamad* in the Bible appears in Genesis, in the account of the Garden of Eden.

Let's take a look.

Scripture:

As we go back to the beginning, we see *hamad* used twice in the account of the Garden of Eden. I've indicated the words that translate *hamad* in bold in the passages below.

READ Genesis 2:8-9, 16-17, and 3:1-8. (It may help you to read all of Genesis 2 and 3 first.) Circle references to *trees* and underline what is said about each tree.

Genesis 2:8-9

8 The LORD God planted a garden toward the east, in Eden; and there He placed the man whom He had formed.

9 Out of the ground the LORD God caused to grow every tree that **is pleasing** to the sight and good for food; the tree of life also in the midst of the garden, and the tree of the knowledge of good and evil.

Genesis 2:16-17

16 The LORD God commanded the man, saying, "From any tree of the garden you may eat freely;

17 but from the tree of the knowledge of good and evil you shall not eat, for in the day that you eat from it you will surely die."

Genesis 3:1-8

1 Now the serpent was more crafty than any beast of the field which the LORD God had made. And he said to the woman, "Indeed, has God said, 'You shall not eat from any tree of the garden'?"

2 The woman said to the serpent, "From the fruit of the trees of the garden we may eat;

3 but from the fruit of the tree which is in the middle of the garden, God has said, 'You shall not eat from it or touch it, or you will die.'"

4 The serpent said to the woman, "You surely will not die!

5 "For God knows that in the day you eat from it your eyes will be opened, and you will be like God, knowing good and evil."

> 6 When the woman saw that the tree was good for food, and that it was a delight to the eyes, and that the tree **was desirable** to make one wise, she took from its fruit and ate; and she gave also to her husband with her, and he ate.
>
> 7 Then the eyes of both of them were opened, and they knew that they were naked; and they sewed fig leaves together and made themselves loin coverings.
>
> 8 They heard the sound of the LORD God walking in the garden in the cool of the day, and the man and his wife hid themselves from the presence of the LORD God among the trees of the garden.

Reason through the Scriptures:

What does God do in Genesis 2:8-9?

What trees are mentioned and how are they described?

Compare the use of *hamad* ("is pleasing" and "was desirable" in the text above) to its use in the tenth commandment found in Exodus 20:17 ("covet"). What do you learn about the usage of this word from these occurrences? Explain.

According to Genesis 2:16-17, what does God command the man with regard to the trees?

Living Content in a Material World

Lesson Two
The Desire for More, the Beauty of Less

How is the serpent described in Genesis 3:1? What does he ask the woman? What do you think of the way he phrases the question?

How does the woman respond? How does this compare with Genesis 2:17?

How does the serpent contradict God's truth? What does he tell her and what does he imply about God?

What is the woman's path to disobedience? Follow the verbs.

What results when the woman and man disobey God?

Let's take a step back. What was Adam and Eve's situation like to start with? What was available to them? How would you describe their original relationship to God?

How did the serpent's "counter-offer" compare with what God had already provided?

How did seeking "more" turn out for them?

Adam and Eve fell for the oldest lie in the book that began with a simple doubt-inducing question: *Did God really say?* The serpent called into question God's commandment and goodness suggesting that He was holding out on something good! Rather than choose to submit to God's command, the man and the woman ate from the tree that they thought offered them moral autonomy—knowing good and evil. Up to this point, of course, they didn't know evil, they only knew good.

Who is the functional boss in your life? Who decides what you do, when, and how? How does your view affect your relationship to both people and things?

What good and pleasing things has God blessed you with? How are you doing at being grateful for and tending those? What are you valuing more highly, the gift or the Giver?

Are you content? We'll look at this more in coming weeks, but for today, just think about your level of contentment and jot down how you're doing in this department. As we move forward, pay attention to what feeds both contentment and discontent in your life.

Western culture cultivates and feeds coveting. We all know this. The machine is powerful and unrelenting. Years ago, I found that my desire for newer and shinier all but stopped when I gave up mall walking and window shopping. Turned out when I fixed my eyes in a different direction I had far fewer "needs."

Temptation, though, like a virus mutates and pursues. Now, a simple click to research a product online results in that product—and its friends—following me. My Google search results in a Google chase as Google ads pursue me for, I don't even know how long! Screens do not cause sin, but they wake up sins of many stripes in many people. Maybe you relate.

It's possible that you no longer have an active struggle with coveting. Over the years, God may have healed and restored in that area of your life. You may have all but stopped the influx. You may not be bringing more in, but sin has an ugly way of leaving consequences in its path.

And, yes, there are other reasons for accumulation—inheritances, hand-me-downs, gifts, and the list goes on—we'll address more of them as we move along. For now, though, let's think through what material desires in our lives run counter to God.

Take some time to write a prayer below asking God to guide you in this process and to reveal hidden sin that you may not even be aware of. If you're not sure what to pray, read Psalm 139 and let it encourage and help you.

The Original Biblical Minimalist

Have you ever looked at John the Baptist with pure envy? Yes, I know he lived in the wilderness and lost his head to a crazy king, but the man never had to wrestle with the age-old question, "What's for dinner?", and he never lost sleep over "What outfit should I wear tomorrow?".

Obviously, John did not set out to be a minimalist nor would he have defined himself as such. His job was clear: prepare the way of the Lord, make His paths straight, preach a baptism of repentance for the forgiveness of sins (Mark 1:2-4). Mark mentions his clothing to point the reader back to the account of Elijah in 2 Kings 1:8.

John's whole life pointed to Jesus and we can learn from his example what a whole-hearted, single-eyed life of service to God can look like. My shoulders are actually loosening and my breathing easing as I'm thinking about this possibility!

Scripture:

While we will look at passages from Mark and John, Luke gives us the most complete history of John the Baptist. You can read about his parents, the announcement of his birth, and more of his life beginning in Luke 1.

Note that the capitalized words in the following passage indicate that they are quotations from the Old Testament. I've indicated in parenthesis the passages that Mark quotes.

READ Mark 1:1-8 and mark every reference to *John the Baptist* including synonyms and pronouns.

> *Mark 1:1-8*
>
> 1 The beginning of the gospel of Jesus Christ, the Son of God.
>
> 2 As it is written in Isaiah the prophet: "BEHOLD, I SEND MY MESSENGER AHEAD OF YOU, WHO WILL PREPARE YOUR WAY; (Malachi 3:1)
>
> 3 THE VOICE OF ONE CRYING IN THE WILDERNESS, 'MAKE READY THE WAY OF THE LORD, MAKE HIS PATHS STRAIGHT.' " (Isaiah 40:3)
>
> 4 John the Baptist appeared in the wilderness preaching a baptism of repentance for the forgiveness of sins.
>
> 5 And all the country of Judea was going out to him, and all the people of Jerusalem; and they were being baptized by him in the Jordan River, confessing their sins.
>
> 6 John was clothed with camel's hair and wore a leather belt around his waist, and his diet was locusts and wild honey.

Living Content in a Material World

Lesson Two
The Desire for More, the Beauty of Less

> 7 And he was preaching, and saying, "After me One is coming who is mightier than I, and I am not fit to stoop down and untie the thong of His sandals.
>
> 8 "I baptized you with water; but He will baptize you with the Holy Spirit."

Reason through the Scriptures:

According to verse 1, who is the focus of Mark's gospel account and what is significant about Him?

Who is John the Baptist and where is he? What was prophesied about him?

What message does he proclaim? What else does he do?

How far is his message reaching? How many people are responding?

What does he eat on Tuesdays? on Saturdays? What does he wear on Mondays? on Thursdays?

How much time do you invest in acquiring/choosing/tending clothing? Just asking . . .

How much time do you spend thinking about, acquiring and preparing food? Just asking . . .

Now, let's think about what opportunities you are pre-empting if you're prioritizing the acquiring, tending, and organizing of your stuff. Who is getting less of you? What could you be doing with that time? (REMEMBER, I'm letting the Word cut into me; take this only as personally as the Spirit is working it in your life. I'm dealing in application here to my life in particular.)

Do you ever feel wearied by the constant stream of decisions that you face daily? If so, what toll is that taking on you?

How would your typical day be different if you had less decisions and less complexity? Take a moment and describe what you think it would be like and how you would feel.

I, for one, am weary of decisions. I avoid places like Subway because there are too many questions: *What sandwich on what bread? Toasted or not? What extras? What sauces? Do you want to make it a combo?* I DON'T KNOW!!! Would someone just give me a cheese pizza?!

The older I get, the more I know the Word of God and the God of the Word, the more convinced I become that less stuff and less options mean more life. Let's face it, it's easier for me to fix my eyes on Jesus when I'm not constantly hunting for my lost glasses amid the clutter.

Scripture:

Before we wrap up this week, let's look at one more John the Baptist account and consider the general trajectory of his life.

READ John 3:22-30 and mark every reference to *Jesus* and every reference to *John*.

John 3:22-30

22 After these things Jesus and His disciples came into the land of Judea, and there He was spending time with them and baptizing.

23 John also was baptizing in Aenon near Salim, because there was much water there; and people were coming and were being baptized—

24 for John had not yet been thrown into prison.

25 Therefore there arose a discussion on the part of John's disciples with a Jew about purification.

26 And they came to John and said to him, "Rabbi, He who was with you beyond the Jordan, to whom you have testified, behold, He is baptizing and all are coming to Him."

27 John answered and said, "A man can receive nothing unless it has been given him from heaven.

28 "You yourselves are my witnesses that I said, 'I am not the Christ,' but, 'I have been sent ahead of Him.'

29 "He who has the bride is the bridegroom; but the friend of the bridegroom, who stands and hears him, rejoices greatly because of the bridegroom's voice. So this joy of mine has been made full.

30 "He must increase, but I must decrease.

Lesson Two
The Desire for More, the Beauty of Less

Bigger Barns

Reason through the Scriptures:

Look back at where you marked references to John and to Jesus and, using the chart below, compare what you learned about each.

John   **Jesus**

Summarize what changes for John when Jesus enters the scene.

According to verse 26, what are John's disciples concerned about?

How does John respond to them? Why?

What has John's entire life been about? How do his priorities support his mission?

Living Content in a Material World

Lesson Two
The Desire for More, the Beauty of Less

What is *your* life about? Do *your* priorities align with your mission? If so, how? If not, what changes are in order?

How does John describe his joy in verse 29? Do you think it surprised his disciples? Explain.

According to verse 24, what will eventually happen to John? You can read how John's story ends in Matthew 14 and Mark 6.

How does John describe his life compared to Jesus in verse 30? How does this compare with what human nature desires?

Is Jesus increasing in your life? If not, what is and why is it?

More of One, Less of Another

Finite. Like it or not we have limits. More of one thing, means less of another. More clutter, more stuff means less time for God, family, and everything else. Better organization can help, but eventually we all run into capacity.

I have so much more to say on this . . . capacity for relationships, the 24-hour limits of a day, and on and on, but you know what? Lessons have an optimum capacity, too, and I'm rapidly reaching the edges of this one. So, let's move on.

Continuing Forward

With two lessons and one week of actual decluttering in the books, there are so many ways this adventure could go sideways. Having traveled this path before, I know (and have fallen into!) numerous potholes along the way. Most of my issues have to do with perfectionism: *If I can't do it perfectly, I won't do it at all* kind of thinking.

Sometimes my problems come from entitlement sloth. I've made that one up, clearly, but let me explain. When I'm overtaxed in one area—say writing—I tend to let other areas slide. Overdoing in one area often correlates with underdoing in another. It all probably goes back to capacity in some way, now that I think about it. Please know this is not an excuse, it's just an observation. You may relate.

Why bring up my issues? Because I know that at this point, we are all faced with yet another decision and what we do going forward will likely be tied with how we think and what we do with how we think.

Right now, you face three basic choices if you didn't finish your kitchen last week.

Bail . . .

Likely, at some point in the past we've all done this or we wouldn't be in this study together right now. You're an adult and you can bail out. You can look around your kitchen and decide that you didn't make enough progress this week, that your situation is hopeless, and go back and sit on the couch. You're an adult, bailing is an option. I think it's a terrible option, but it is an option.

Stay . . .

My guess is that staying in the kitchen—"just until I'm done"—is your most likely temptation. It sure is mine! I know the voices in my head are loud . . . yours likely are, too! You can read mine below and add yours to them.

"Finish it now or you won't finish it at all . . ."

"I didn't do it perfectly, so it's not good enough . . ."

"I still stink at this! I have to stay here until I figure it out . . ."

"   "

"   "

"   "

Keep Moving . . .

I'm not going to lie. This is hard for me, too. If you didn't finish this week's room, just tidy as best you can and move on to the next area. I learned this from organizational expert Peter Walsh. If you get ahead in future weeks, you can go back and continue to work where we've been. More likely, you'll want to run through the house more than once.

As a writer, I think of this as something of a first draft. We are going for the big problems and aiming at "good enough" results this time through.

Continue with 15 minutes a day this week moving to your home's main living space, likely your living and/or family rooms. Again, as you work, listen to your audio Bible to help pace your work and remind you of why you're in this process.

Decide now that you won't go into declutter mode in other rooms. If you do, you're likely to stir up a pile of mess that will discourage you even more. You will be able to think more clearly and with more focus when you keep your head in one place. Soon you'll begin to see real progress that will help spur you on to more!

Reviewing the Progress

Week 1—Kitchen / Dining

What we (not the royal "we," but the "we" of you in submission to God) accomplished:

What remains:

Lesson Two
The Desire for More, the Beauty of Less

Bigger Barns

What made me laugh:

This is what made me laugh: puppy teeth in a jewelry box from my 6-year old Great Dane that found in a kitchen drawer. There's more to that story, but we'll have to save for another day!

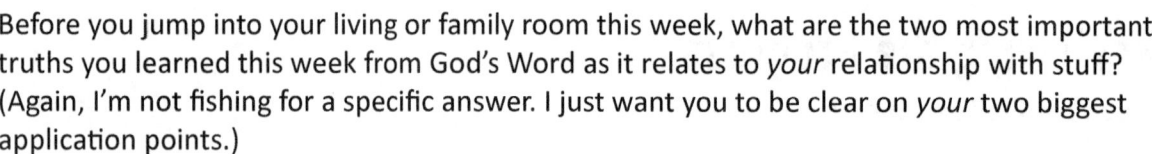

Week 2—Main Living Space—Living / Family Room — YOU ARE HERE

Week 3—Master Bedroom

Week 4—Other Bedrooms

Week 5—Office

Week 6—Bathrooms / Laundry

Before you jump into your living or family room this week, what are the two most important truths you learned this week from God's Word as it relates to *your* relationship with stuff? (Again, I'm not fishing for a specific answer. I just want you to be clear on *your* two biggest application points.)

1.

2.

Remember, if you hit a wall as you're working, review your takeaways truths, and let God's truth take you over, around, or through it.

As you work through your living room or family room this week, continue using your audio Bible to go wide in God's Word in at least 15-minute increments. You may find that 15 minutes at a time is not enough for you. If you're still feeling fresh after 15, keep going until you feel a stall and then call it a day or at least take a break.

If you finish listening to the gospel of Matthew, either start the gospel of Mark, or listen to what Solomon has to say about "all of the things" in Ecclesiastes.

Each day, jot down something simple you'd like to remember from what you heard. This is just to help you stay engaged in your listening. We want the audio Bible to be more than just background noise.

Day 1

Day 2

Day 3

Day 4

Day 5

Day 6

Day 7

Lesson Two
The Desire for More, the Beauty of Less

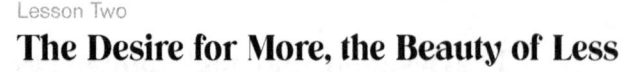

We all have different capacities for what we can manage and I am certainly not promoting asceticism here. That said, as far as rubber-meets-the-road application in my life, I'm finding that more stuff equates with less time for what matters most and conversely, the less stuff I pack into my life, the more time I have for God and others.

WANT MORE TIME? CONSIDER LESS STUFF

LESSON THREE

Extracting the Precious

DON'T MISPLACE THE PRECIOUS!

We had a standing joke in our house when I was growing up. Whenever my Mom couldn't find something, she'd say, "Oh no, I've put it in a safe place!" The safer the place, the longer we looked for it. To this day, we still laugh about the important things in the safe places!

Important things call for safe places, right? Consider your passport, your keys, the birth certificates, the credit cards—and the list goes on. When you need them, you want to know their exact location. When you're out of the house, though, you want them to be secure. And so the dilemma: *How do I remember where the important lives when it doesn't live in plain sight?* Now, if the organized people were reading this, they would have simple answers involving file cabinets and safes and whatnot, but I suspect *you* are picking up what I'm putting down or we wouldn't be doing this study together! Actually, that's probably the wrong metaphor here, but I digress.

We are not alone! Studies show that the average American spends 2.5 days a year looking for lost items—math says that's about a half-a-year over an average lifetime.

In our culture of material abundance, it's easy to lose the important and precious in the midst of the common and worthless both literally and figuratively. Let's see what God's Word has to say about this human propensity and the better path God calls us to walk.

Studying Inductively and Applying Truth

As we begin our week with the prophet Jeremiah, I want to review the principles of inductive Bible study.

As we study the Scripture, we first slow down and **Observe** the text carefully. Our goal is to simply find out what the text says. We may run across some head-scratching phrases, but at this point, we simply observe and allow ourselves to shrug our shoulders if we don't immediately understand.

After we've taken our time and observed the text well, we begin to **Interpret** or try to understand what the text means. Specifically, we try to understand what the original author intended for his original audience to understand. We're looking for one answer from the text, not an existential, "What it means to me."

In order to interpret the text, we pay attention to the context (the verses around the passage we're looking at), cross-references, word studies, and the overall teaching of Scripture knowing that Scripture interprets Scripture and will not contradict itself.

Once we've determined to the best of our ability what the text means, we begin to **Apply** the text in our own lives. This is where we will see many applications can come out of the one meaning of the text as we apply the truth or principle to different life situations.

What we will see in this passage is a general principle that we can apply to the process that we are in together.

The Precious and the Worthless

One of the most quoted verses of Scripture comes from Jeremiah 29:11: "'For I know the plans that I have for you,' declares the LORD, 'plans for welfare and not for calamity to give you a future and a hope.'" Most people entirely miss the context. This is not a feel-good verse and Jeremiah is not a feel-good book. In fact in this oft-merchandised verse, God tells Judah to make themselves at home in their Babylonian captivity, because they'll be there for seventy years. This verse offers hope not in the middle of hardship, but *in the middle of judgment.*

Today we'll look at a portion of Jeremiah 15, so let me set you in context. In this chapter we see a picture of the people God will judge, with the LORD saying that even if Moses or Samuel prayed for them, God would still bring judgment. In this dire situation, Jeremiah laments his own birth. After all, who wants to be the one to bring news of judgment to this kind of people?! You think social media is a mean-spirited jungle? I don't think we can even imagine what Jeremiah faced. And so we come to our text today . . .

Bigger Barns Living Content in a Material World

Lesson Three
Extracting the Precious

Scripture:

In the passage below, Jeremiah and the LORD dialogue. Jeremiah is the speaker as the passage opens.

READ Jeremiah 15:15-21 and mark references to *Jeremiah* and to the *LORD/God*. Underline references to God speaking *(thus says, declares,* etc.) to help you follow the dialogue.

Jeremiah 15:15-21

15 You who know, O LORD,
   Remember me, take notice of me,
   And take vengeance for me on my persecutors.
   Do not, in view of Your patience, take me away;
   Know that for Your sake I endure reproach.

16 Your words were found and I ate them,
   And Your words became for me a joy and the delight of my heart;
   For I have been called by Your name,
   O LORD God of hosts.

17 I did not sit in the circle of merrymakers,
   Nor did I exult.
   Because of Your hand upon me I sat alone,
   For You filled me with indignation.

18 Why has my pain been perpetual
   And my wound incurable, refusing to be healed?
   Will You indeed be to me like a deceptive stream
   With water that is unreliable?

19 Therefore, thus says the LORD,
   "If you return, then I will restore you—
   Before Me you will stand;
   And if you extract the precious from the worthless,
   You will become My spokesman.
   They for their part may turn to you,
   But as for you, you must not turn to them.

20 "Then I will make you to this people
   A fortified wall of bronze;
   And though they fight against you,
   They will not prevail over you; For I am with you to save you
   And deliver you," declares the LORD.

21 "So I will deliver you from the hand of the wicked, And I will redeem you from the grasp of the violent."

For more context, start by reading all of Jeremiah 15.

Reason through the Scriptures:

What did you learn about Jeremiah from his description of himself and his situation in verses 15-18?

What does Jeremiah ask God for? Why does he say God should answer?

Can you relate with Jeremiah? If so, how? What do you think of his cries to God? Be honest.

How does Jeremiah question God starting in verse 18? What does he say about his own pain and about God's reliability? What do you make of that?

How does God respond to him? What two things does God tell Jeremiah to do in verse 19 and what does He say will happen in response.

If you   then

If you   [then]

Lesson Three
Extracting the Precious

Let's face it. When we speak of "precious" and "worthless" we all have certain images and ideas that immediately pop into our heads. If we're honest, much of our struggle roots in our inability to determine what is truly precious and what is worthless. Many of us have basements and closets packed to the brim because we've mislabled "Worthless" as "Precious" and it has eaten away at not only our time but our hearts as well.

In order to understand what "extracting the precious from the worthless" means in context, and based on that how we can apply it, it will be helpful to look at some of the Hebrew words in the text.

Let's look specifically at these words from verse 19:

> "And if you extract the **precious** (Hebrew: yaqar) from the **worthless**
>   (Hebrew: zalal),
>
> You will become My spokesman."

Precious

There are many resources available to help you with a word study. An easy place to start, however, is with a concordance search to see where else the word is used in the Bible and in what context. Take some time to look closer at the word "precious." You can use whichever tools you prefer to see how the Hebrew word is used elsewhere in the Old Testament.

1 Samuel 3:1

Proverbs 3:13-15

Summarize what you learned about the Hebrew *yaqar*, precious.

Worthless

Again, you can find more info about the Hebrew word, in this case *zalal,* by using any of your favorite resources. Don't freak out when the first thing you see is the verb "shake." We'll circle back around to that in a little bit.

For now, look at how the word *zalal* is translated in Jeremiah 15:19 and elsewhere in the Old Testament by using a concordance. What is it a picture of? Does it resonate with any of the issues of our day? Explain.

We see a principle in Jeremiah 15:19 that even among God's people, the precious and the worthless have a tendency to co-mingle. In the case of Jeremiah himself, his own empty words carried none of the weight of the precious and powerful Word of God. He needed to refocus, to extract the true and precious truth of God's Word from the dross of his own thinking. Only then would he be able to be God's mouthpiece to the people.

Considering what you've learned about *precious* and *worthless* today, what is truly precious in your life? Is anything worth holding onto that would compromise the truly precious?

What's Shaking?

Now let's take a moment to consider the other sense of *zalal,* that is, "to shake." First, let me be clear that we need to be very careful here. One of the more typical errors I see people make in Bible study is taking secondary or tertiary meanings of words and injecting them into a text.

Let me explain. If, for instance, I tried to tell you that there was a connection between "fall" (as in autumn) and "fall" (as in trip), I sure hope you'd call "shenanigans" on me. Clearly, the context will show that these are simply homonyms—words with the *same* spelling but *different* meanings.

Other times, though, we see some connection between alternate word definitions that bear up under scrutiny as we look at the whole counsel of God's Word. I think we have that here with *zalal*. Why is this important? Again, because we often have a hard time *practically* defining "worthless"—at least I do and I'm guessing you're not exempt. Remember, we are living in times when right is being called wrong and wrong is being called right all around us, all the time. Our time, like the time of the judges, is characterized by everyone doing what is right in their own eyes.

Come with me for a moment to the New Testament book of Hebrews. Remember, we are shifting from Hebrew to Greek, so this is **not** an apples to apples comparison. I'm taking you to a cross-reference that I believe runs on the same train of thought. (Haggai—quoted below—uses a different Hebrew word for "to shake" [*raas*, not *zalal*], but I believe we are dealing in synonyms.)

Scripture:

As we come to this passage from the end of Hebrews 12, the author of Hebrews has been looking back to examples of faith in Hebrews 11 and exhorting his readers to look forward and fix their eyes on Jesus as they (and we!) look forward to the heavenly Jerusalem and the city of the living God.

READ Hebrews 12:25-29 and mark references to *shook/shake/shaken*.

Hebrews 12:25-29

25 See to it that you do not refuse Him who is speaking. For if those did not escape when they refused him who warned them on earth, much less will we escape who turn away from Him who warns from heaven.

26 And His voice shook the earth then, but now He has promised, saying, "YET ONCE MORE I WILL SHAKE NOT ONLY THE EARTH, BUT ALSO THE HEAVEN." (Haggai 2:6)

27 This expression, "Yet once more," denotes the removing of those things which can be shaken, as of created things, so that those things which cannot be shaken may remain.

28 Therefore, since we receive a kingdom which cannot be shaken, let us show gratitude, by which we may offer to God an acceptable service with reverence and awe;

29 for our God is a consuming fire.

Reason through the Scriptures:

What did you learn from marking references to *shook/shake/shaken*?

Lesson Three
Extracting the Precious

Bigger Barns

What will last?

What are we going to receive and how is it described?

What is our attitude to be?

What are we to offer to God?

Why do you think we give such weight and importance to things that, as the author of Hebrews would say, can be shaken?

When you consider physical items, are there any that prompt gratitude in your heart toward God? If so, how?

What is something in your life that is worthless that you treat as precious? What truth can you apply to help you think rightly about it?

Lost in the House of God

When Josiah—son of Amon and grandson of Manasseh—enters the biblical narrative as the boy-king of Judah, the northern Kingdom of Israel has already been conquered and scattered by the Assyrians, and Judah stands poised for divine judgment in the wake of King Manasseh's despicable reign.

Known for shedding "much innocent blood" (2 Kings 21:16) as a result of child sacrifice, Manasseh not only led Judah into horrific sin, but also set up idol worship in the very house of the LORD in Jerusalem (2 Kings 21:4ff).

Scripture:

Josiah became king after his father's servants assassinated his father Amon and installed the boy in his father's place. We'll look both at 2 Chronicles which was written for the exiles returning from Babylon and a parallel passage from 2 Kings as we unearth his life story.

READ 2 Chronicles 34:1-7 and 2 Kings 22:1-13. Mark references to *Josiah* and to *the book*.

2 Chronicles 34:1-7

1 *Josiah was eight years old when he became king, and he reigned thirty-one years in Jerusalem.*

2 *He did right in the sight of the LORD, and walked in the ways of his father David and did not turn aside to the right or to the left.*

3 *For in the eighth year of his reign while he was still a youth, he began to seek the God of his father David; and in the twelfth year he began to purge Judah and Jerusalem of the high places, the Asherim, the carved images and the molten images.*

4 *They tore down the altars of the Baals in his presence, and the incense altars that were high above them he chopped down; also the Asherim, the carved images and the molten images he broke in pieces and ground to powder and scattered it on the graves of those who had sacrificed to them.*

5   Then he burned the bones of the priests on their altars and purged Judah and Jerusalem.

6   In the cities of Manasseh, Ephraim, Simeon, even as far as Naphtali, in their surrounding ruins,

7   he also tore down the altars and beat the Asherim and the carved images into powder, and chopped down all the incense altars throughout the land of Israel. Then he returned to Jerusalem.

2 Kings 22:1-13

1   Josiah was eight years old when he became king, and he reigned thirty-one years in Jerusalem; and his mother's name was Jedidah the daughter of Adaiah of Bozkath.

2   He did right in the sight of the LORD and walked in all the way of his father David, nor did he turn aside to the right or to the left.

3   Now in the eighteenth year of King Josiah, the king sent Shaphan, the son of Azaliah the son of Meshullam the scribe, to the house of the LORD saying,

4   "Go up to Hilkiah the high priest that he may count the money brought in to the house of the LORD which the doorkeepers have gathered from the people.

5   "Let them deliver it into the hand of the workmen who have the oversight of the house of the LORD, and let them give it to the workmen who are in the house of the LORD to repair the damages of the house,

6   to the carpenters and the builders and the masons and for buying timber and hewn stone to repair the house.

7   "Only no accounting shall be made with them for the money delivered into their hands, for they deal faithfully."

8   Then Hilkiah the high priest said to Shaphan the scribe, "I have found the book of the law in the house of the LORD." And Hilkiah gave the book to Shaphan who read it.

9   Shaphan the scribe came to the king and brought back word to the king and said, "Your servants have emptied out the money that was found in the house, and have delivered it into the hand of the workmen who have the oversight of the house of the LORD."

10 Moreover, Shaphan the scribe told the king saying, "Hilkiah the priest has given me a book." And Shaphan read it in the presence of the king.

11 When the king heard the words of the book of the law, he tore his clothes.

12 Then the king commanded Hilkiah the priest, Ahikam the son of Shaphan, Achbor the son of Micaiah, Shaphan the scribe, and Asaiah the king's servant saying,

13 "Go, inquire of the LORD for me and the people and all Judah concerning the words of this book that has been found, for great is the wrath of the LORD that burns against us, because our fathers have not listened to the words of this book, to do according to all that is written concerning us."

Reason through the Scriptures:

Briefly describe Josiah. Look where you marked references to him and make a simple list of what you learned.

Using the information that you have, make a simple time line of his life showing when major events occur.

What does Josiah undertake in his eighteenth year, according to 2 Kings 22:3ff?

What does Hilkiah the priest discover in the house of the LORD during the repairs?

What do they do with the book and how does King Josiah respond?

Read Deuteronomy 17:14-20. What was every king of Israel to do? How does this compare with what we've read from 2 Kings 22?

What had God's people lost and where had they lost it?

Have you ever "lost" the Word of God in the midst of your stuff and activities? If so, what did it take for you to recognize that it was gone?

What would it take for you to make adequate "room" for it? What is it that needs to go? This clutter may not be physical—it may be clutter on the calendar, in relationships, or somewhere else! (By the way, don't just take your own word on the solution. Spend some time in prayer asking God.)

When something usurps first place in my life, I have an idol problem. When something usurps first place in your life, you do, too. The people of Judah lost the Word of God in the house of God as a result of blatant and ugly idolatry. Our modern idolatry may not be as blatant but make no mistake, idolatry is always ugly.

Living Content in a Material World

Lesson Three
Extracting the Precious

Hidden Treasures and Precious Pearls

We've already seen that Jesus told His disciples to send their treasures ahead, but what else does He teach about precious and worthless things?

Scripture:

In Matthew 13 Jesus tells a series of parables explaining what the kingdom of heaven is like. Here are two of them in just three verses! Talk about efficiency!

READ Matthew 13:44-46 and mark references to the *kingdom of heaven*.

> *Matthew 13:44-46*
>
> 44 *"The kingdom of heaven is like a treasure hidden in the field, which a man found and hid again; and from joy over it he goes and sells all that he has and buys that field.*
>
> 45 *"Again, the kingdom of heaven is like a merchant seeking fine pearls,*
>
> 46 *and upon finding one pearl of great value, he went and sold all that he had and bought it.*

Reason through the Scriptures:

What two similes does Jesus use to describe the kingdom of heaven? What does He say the kingdom is like?

What happens in the first parable? What does the man find? What does he do and with what emotion does he do it?

What does his emotion tell us about the value of the treasure versus the value of all that he sold?

Lesson Three
Extracting the Precious

What happens in the second parable? What is the merchant seeking and what does he find?

How does he respond to the opportunity of the one great pearl?

According to these parables, what is this mysterious kingdom of God worth? Can anything compare?

If you have possessions that are interfering with your ability to live with a kingdom mindset, are you able to let them go with joy? Explain.

Questions I'm Asking Myself

This past week, I stumbled on a fascinating website where people post pictures of what they would take out of their houses in the event of a fire. It's a unique twist on the *"What one item would you save from a fire"* ice breaker that most of us have answered at some point in our lives.

Fire forces the issue from two fronts: 1. *What can you decide on quickly?* and 2. *What can you carry?* If you can't carry everything that you fancy, you will carry what you value most.

As we move through this process together, I'm finding questions to ask myself about my stuff that help me to practically hold it up to God's Word. The question that I'm using today is a more nuanced variation on the "fire" scenario. No promises on whether or not it will help you, but it is helping me to think through the stuff and to sift and separate what is earthly "precious" from what is truly worthless and to think more clearly about the items that fall somewhere in between.

So here we go . . .

If you went on vacation and came home to the news that everything in your house had been consumed by fire, blown away by hurricane, washed away by tsunami—you fill in your local danger—what physical items would fit into the following categories? Explanations of the categories are below!

Thrilled!   **Relieved**   **Won't Miss**   **Will Replace**   **Heartbroken!**

Thrilled!

These are items that should be gone. You know it, but you haven't gotten around to it. Perhaps (and likely!) it's something that someone else in the house won't let go—an 80's-era turntable, for instance.

This is the stuff that hangs around even though it has no business being in your house. None.

If these items disappeared, you would do a little dance . . . even if you were raised Baptist! Seriously.

Relieved

These are items that you need to let go, but for some reason you can't. If you woke up one day to find them gone you wouldn't dance and you might even feel a little remorse, but mostly you'd feel relief.

They are items you think either have some monetary value or they have an emotional hook in you. You know they need to go, but you can't for the life of you figure out what to do with them.

Here are some examples. They are:

- things you think you should be able to turn back into cash.
- things you want to donate to "the right person."
- things that belonged to someone you love, but don't have a place in your life.
- things that belonged to someone you love, but that make you feel bad.
- old paperwork, that you fear you may need "someday."

Won't Miss

If your house burned down tomorrow, you probably wouldn't miss most of what would go up in smoke. People's use of their stuff falls in line with the Pareto principle: we use 20% of our things 80% of the time. Eighty-percent of the commonplace items you will likely not miss on a regular basis, as the 80% you only use 20% of the time.

Will Replace

This leads us to the other 20%. Of this 20%, most of the items you'd simply replace if you lost them in a fire. If you make a mistake in your decluttering, you can also replace it. It is not the end of the world. Remember, if you beat yourself up for every mistake, you will stop moving forward.

Heartbroken!

If your house burned down tomorrow, there's a small fraction of items over which your heart would break. Let's be clear, these ephemeral trinkets are not true treasures, but if we choose well, they will serve to remind us of God's faithfulness in the past and of His good gifts of family and friends. They will also incline our hearts toward heaven rather than anchoring them in this world's brokenness.

Reviewing the Progress

Week 1—Kitchen / Dining

Week 2—Living / Family Room

What we (again, not the royal "we," but the "we" of you in submission to God) accomplished:

What remains:

What made me laugh:

Week 3—Master Bedroom — YOU ARE HERE

Week 4—Other Bedrooms

Week 5—Office

Week 6—Bathrooms / Laundry

As you get about your decluttering, remember the continuum. The columns on the edges should be pretty clear. Those in the middle will be grey, but when all is said and done, they won't matter much.

Thrilled!   **Relieved**   **Won't Miss**   **Will Replace**   **Heartbroken!**

When you find yourself stalled at some point this week in your process, ask yourself this question:

What obedience is this stuff holding me back from? What would I be free to do for Christ and His Kingdom if I wasn't shackled to this clutter? Write it down and keep it in the front of your mind.

Lesson Three
Extracting the Precious

Bigger Barns

Work through your master bedroom this week continuing to use your audio Bible to go wide in God's Word in at least 15-minute increments. If you've finished Matthew and Mark, move on to Luke.

Each day, jot down something simple you'd like to remember from what you heard. Again, this is just to help you stay engaged, not the basis for a doctoral dissertation.

Day 1

Day 2

Day 3

Day 4

Day 5

Day 6

Day 7

DON'T WASTE YOUR LIFE ON THE WORTHLESS!

LESSON FOUR

Disorder and Every Evil Thing

NOT A GOD OF CONFUSION, BUT OF PEACE

And now we are going to get into my business and wrestle and struggle. We're not going to sprinkle Bible verses on my thoughts of how to get to the bottom of my stuff . . . because if you've ever been in my house, you know my thoughts don't work. I need surgery, the surgery only God's Word can provide.

Because I'm a creative and the people I love are creatives, I don't particularly like this lesson. In fact, I'm having a tough time even putting this on paper because I think my sin nature has a deep root at this place.

All this to say, if you're offended . . . know that I have the scalpel poised to cut the disease out of my heart, not yours. Enough evading let's go.

Lesson Four
Disorder and Every Evil Thing

Two Ways to Swing and Miss in Bible Study

As I've been struggling through the process of obeying God with my stuff, I've been contemplating the two main ways to swing and miss in Bible study with regard to application. Let me explain.

1. "What it means to me" thinking. Although many people use imprecise language when they actually mean to say, "This is how I'm applying the clear meaning of the text," those who think the meaning of the Word changes like the weather, leave themselves open to every wind of doctrine. The Word means what it means regardless of whether you or I ever hear it. Its meaning isn't dependent on a hearer.

"What it means to me" thinking is unanchored, egocentric, and ultimately lacking in power as it seeks to impose meaning onto (*eisegesis*) the text of Scripture as opposed to drawing the meaning and subsequent application out of what is there (*exegesis*).

2. Trite or dabbed-on truths. How often do we come face to face with the needed chemotherapy of Scripture and yet opt for Bactine and a band-aid? In our zeal not to commit the error of *eisegesis*, we often stop short of taking biblical truth and applying a principle we see to our specific situation.

Remember, the one clear meaning of the text we seek as we interpret and accurately handle the Word of truth (2 Timothy 2:15) can and—if we take God seriously—must be applied to a myriad of individual situations. We can't dodge truth because we think "the Bible doesn't speak to that . . .".

God has given believers everything that pertains to life and godliness (2 Peter 1:3). If we need an answer, we need to look for the principles that God has put in front of us and ask Him for the wisdom to find and apply the proper truths.

Your Pick: Disorder or Peace?

With that, let's head to the book of James and to a cross-reference from 1 Corinthians. Don't worry, we're jumping in *after* the mouth part in James and we're only looking at what 1 Corinthians has to say about God and order in the church, not about prophecy. That, my friends, is another topic for another day!

Lesson Four

Disorder and Every Evil Thing

Living Content in a Material World

Scripture:

A gut-punch chapter in a gut-punch book, James 3 has already been addressing the human mouth problem by the time we arrive at our text in James 3:13-18. We're paying close attention in these passages to the Greek word *akatastasia*—translated *disorder* in James 3 and *confusion* in 1 Corinthians 14. But lest you think we're getting off easy with just *disorder*, James also has something to say about gentleness, mercy, peace . . . and I need to stop telling you and let you look at the Word for yourself!

READ James 3:13-18 and mark all references to *wise/wisdom*. **READ** it a second time and cross through each instance of *wisdom* that references earthly wisdom. Finally, mark *disorder*, or if you're playing in Greek, *akatastasia*.

James 3:13-18

13 *Who among you is wise and understanding? Let him show by his good behavior his deeds in the gentleness of wisdom.*

14 *But if you have bitter jealousy and selfish ambition in your heart, do not be arrogant and so lie against the truth.*

15 *This wisdom is not that which comes down from above, but is earthly, natural, demonic.*

16 *For where jealousy and selfish ambition exist, there is disorder and every evil thing.*

17 *But the wisdom from above is first pure, then peaceable, gentle, reasonable, full of mercy and good fruits, unwavering, without hypocrisy.*

18 *And the seed whose fruit is righteousness is sown in peace by those who make peace.*

READ 1 Corinthians 14:29-33 and mark references to *God* and to *confusion* (Greek: *akatastasia*).

1 Corinthians 14:29-33

29 *Let two or three prophets speak, and let the others pass judgment.*

30 *But if a revelation is made to another who is seated, the first one must keep silent.*

31 *For you can all prophesy one by one, so that all may learn and all may be exhorted;*

32 *and the spirits of prophets are subject to prophets;*

33 *for God is not a God of confusion but of peace, as in all the churches of the saints.*

Reason through the Scriptures:

Who is James addressing in his letter? What about Paul? Who is he writing to?

Let's focus our attention on James. What big contrast does he address?

What characterizes true wisdom? If you're not sure how to get that wisdom, check out what James advises in James 1:5-8.

By contrast, what characterizes earthly wisdom?

How have you needed wisdom in this whole process of decluttering and dealing with your stuff? Have you asked God for His wisdom yet? It may seem trivial, but it is not. God wants to give wisdom to those who need it! Remember James 1:5-8.

Living Content in a Material World

Lesson Four
Disorder and Every Evil Thing

Did you notice the word in verse 16 that is a bedfellow with "every evil thing"? Write it down below.

Based on the context, what kind of "disorder" do you think James is talking about here?

Now, let's look at the use of the same Greek word (*akatastasia*) in 1 Corinthians 14:33 and consider the context of that passage. What general issue does Paul address in 1 Corinthians 14:29-33?

If someone instructs a group to take turns, what likely has been going on? What is the problem? What is Paul looking to restore?

Briefly compare how Paul and James use *akastastasia*.

In contrast to what is happening at Corinth, how does Paul describe God in 1 Corinthians 14:33?

Now, I want you to think through what you know about God from what He has revealed about Himself in the Bible and compare this with 1 Corinthians 14:33. If you're not sure, let these passages prompt you:

• Genesis 1–2   • Exodus 25–40   • Leviticus   • Numbers 1–10   • Ezekiel 40–48

Just by glancing over the content in these passages—and, no, I'm not expecting you to read all of Leviticus to answer—what do you notice about God?

Now, thinking back to both James' and Paul's use of *akastastasia,* it is clear the context has to do with people and relationships. Disorder and confusion in the people-realm is not of God. And this is where we will make the hermeneutical leap to application, so weigh what I'm saying here.

While the Scriptural usage in these passages relates to people, I think the full counsel of God's Word points to our God as a God of order and the adversary as one who confuses and destroys. Stick with me here and answer this. When the inanimate "members of your household" rise up in rebellion—that is when the stuffed animals are out playing under the tables, when the socks make a trail to your daughter, when dirty dishes crawl up out of your sink like zombies—how does that affect the *people* in the house? Sort of rhetorical, but not really.

Like it or not, for most people environments affect attitudes and relationships. Disorder in environments often causes varying levels of disorder in relationships. Let's think about that for a moment.

How does disorder in your home affect you personally?

Living Content in a Material World

Lesson Four
Disorder and Every Evil Thing

How does disorder affect those you live with and your relationship with them?

Does thinking of "disorder" as destructive change your perspective on it? If so, why and how?

I know, you're reaching for the matches right now, aren't you? "Mama can take care of this problem out back right quick!"

Honestly, that's where I wanted to head with James! "DISORDER AND EVERY EVIL THING!! BURN IT ALL!!" But James has so much more to say that will affect *how* we deal with disorder. Buckle in and remember, I'm preaching to myself first and foremost and I sure wasn't looking for *this* when I came to the text. God's Word is funny that way—just when you think you've got that sword in a box, the other edge comes for you!

Okay, back to James for a story problem. (I know, you thought story problems only existed in math class. Nope!)

Pam is cleaning out the basement and finds an old—and in her opinion "worthless"—turntable. (Kids, the turntable is the great, great grandfather of the modern MP3.) She wants to throw it in the bonfire, but her hubby loves it and has been hanging on to it forever. There is potential conflict brewing. Regardless of whether the answer is "stay" or "go," what actions and attitudes does James 3:17-18 rule out and why?

Which of wisdom's characteristics will you most need to remember and exhibit as you walk the decluttering path with other people in your house? Explain.

I've moved through the stages of trying to get others on board, to passive-aggressive cleaning, and now finally to trying to take care of my own things and helping others as they will accept it and in such a way as to be gentle and helpful. Essentially, I'm starting with the log in my own closet first, so to speak . . .

By now you may be wondering why some of us keep getting ourselves into messes. For a possible answer to that and a framework for next steps, let's go back to the beginning.

The Creation Mandate: Subdue and Rule

The early pages of the Bible lay out the creation narrative that recount God's ordered creation of the world including the cycles of days and seasons and the cycles of work and rest. Let's pick up at the end of Genesis 1 and observe as God creates mankind and gives them a job.

Scripture:

READ Genesis 1:27-28 and mark references to *God* and to *the earth* including pronouns.

Genesis 1:27-28

27 *God created man in His own image, in the image of God He created him; male and female He created them.*

28 *God blessed them; and God said to them, "Be fruitful and multiply, and fill the earth, and subdue it; and rule over the fish of the sea and over the birds of the sky and over every living thing that moves on the earth."*

You know there's more to the Creation story. Read all of Genesis 1 for a refresher.

Reason through the Scriptures:

Look back at where you marked references to God and list everything the text tells us about Him and what He does.

What specifically does God tell the people to do?

Lesson Four
Disorder and Every Evil Thing

What will the people's relationship with the earth be like?

Let's focus on the word *subdue*. What does it mean to *subdue* the earth? What does it take to *subdue* something in a general sense?

There's something about the idea of subduing the earth that is almost (okay, actually) too big for me to wrap my mind around. Is that just me? Probably not. So, let's dial an application back a little bit. Look around the room you're sitting in right now. What would it take for you to subdue it, to be a good manager of your current environment, to bring it under your control? What stands in your way or makes it difficult?

Subdued Before the Lord

Subduing doesn't stop in Genesis. In fact, we see this concept sprinkled throughout the accounts of the people of Israel entering the Promised Land. I'll set up the context of each passage and I encourage you to read the full chapters of Numbers 32, Joshua 18 and 1 Chronicles 22.

Scripture:

In Numbers 32, Moses talks to the men of Reuben and Gad when they want to settle across the Jordan River—in the TransJordan region—away from the rest of Israel.

In Joshua 18:1-4, Joshua urges the seven tribes who haven't settled in the land that God has subdued before them to get with it.

In 1 Chronicles 22:18-19, David talks to his son Solomon about what God has done and what he should do.

Lesson Four
Disorder and Every Evil Thing

Bigger Barns

READ Numbers 32:20-23 and mark references to *you* (referring to the TransJordan tribes) and to the word *subdued*.

Numbers 32:20-23

20 So Moses said to them, "If you will do this, if you will arm yourselves before the LORD for the war,

21 and all of you armed men cross over the Jordan before the LORD until He has driven His enemies out from before Him,

22 and the land is subdued before the LORD, then afterward you shall return and be free of obligation toward the LORD and toward Israel, and this land shall be yours for a possession before the LORD.

23 "But if you will not do so, behold, you have sinned against the LORD, and be sure your sin will find you out.

READ Joshua 18:1-4 and mark references to the *LORD* and *subdued*.

Joshua 18:1-4

1 Then the whole congregation of the sons of Israel assembled themselves at Shiloh, and set up the tent of meeting there; and the land was subdued before them.

2 There remained among the sons of Israel seven tribes who had not divided their inheritance.

3 So Joshua said to the sons of Israel, "How long will you put off entering to take possession of the land which the LORD, the God of your fathers, has given you?

4 "Provide for yourselves three men from each tribe that I may send them, and that they may arise and walk through the land and write a description of it according to their inheritance; then they shall return to me.

READ 1 Chronicles 22:18-19 and mark references to the *LORD* and *subdued*.

2 Chronicles 22:18-19

18 "Is not the LORD your God with you? And has He not given you rest on every side? For He has given the inhabitants of the land into my hand, and the land is subdued before the LORD and before His people.

19 "Now set your heart and your soul to seek the LORD your God; arise, therefore, and build the sanctuary of the LORD God, so that you may bring the ark of the covenant of the LORD and the holy vessels of God into the house that is to be built for the name of the LORD."

Reason through the Scriptures:

What did you learn about the LORD in each of the passages? What role did He play in subduing the land?

Looking at all three passages, summarize what was involved on the part of the people in subduing the land God was giving to them. What shining and not-so-shining moments did they have?

What principles can we learn from them about handling what God has entrusted to us?

Reviewing the Progress

Week 1—Kitchen / Dining

Week 2—Living / Family Room

Week 3—Master Bedroom

What we (again, not the royal "we," but the "we" of you in submission to God) accomplished:

Lesson Four
Disorder and Every Evil Thing

Bigger Barns

What remains:

What was tougher than I thought and the truth I used to overcome it:

Week 4—Other Bedrooms — YOU ARE HERE

Week 5—Office

Week 6—Bathrooms / Laundry

Remember to use the continuum as a guide again this week *if it helps!*

| **Thrilled!** | **Relieved** | **Won't Miss** | **Will Replace** | **Heartbroken!** |

As you work through other bedrooms this week, think about how you can *serve*.

If it's a kid's room, ask yourself *"How can I help my child choose the best so they are not weighed down by things?"*

If it is a guest room, ask *"How can I clear as much out as possible so I can easily extend hospitality? Can I purge the closet more? Can I empty drawers?"*

Go ahead and record your key takeaway from this week's time in the Word and record it below! Keep it simple so you can remember it.

Living Content in a Material World

Lesson Four
Disorder and Every Evil Thing

WIDE

Work through your other bedrooms this week continuing to use your audio Bible to go wide in God's Word in at least 15-minute increments. After finishing Matthew, Mark and Luke, let's stay on the path with Jesus and continue through John.

Remember to jot down something you want to remember each day. Again, this is just to help you stay engaged.

Day 1

Day 2

Day 3

Day 4

Day 5

Day 6

Day 7

SUBDUE THE ROOM!

Lesson Four
Disorder and Every Evil Thing

Bigger Barns

LESSON FIVE

Questions to Ask

STUCK? LET'S ASK SOME HARD AND CLARIFYING QUESTIONS.

Well, here we are. I tried to take a spin through my bedroom this morning (yes, I'm a week behind because I've been writing!!) and while I brought some order to an armoire, I did more shuffling than decluttering. Apparently the technical term for this is "churn"—moving items around, but not moving them out. Now, in my defense, I am on my second pass through the room, but the resistance is harder this time. I've made the easy decisions and now it's getting real. I'm sure you know the feeling. If you don't and you keep marching forward, you will soon enough.

The first round is easy, like a writer's first draft. Get something done, get something out, move fast, and don't linger on the stuff that will be harder and take longer. Still, while the draft is quicker and easier and can push hard decisions down the road—yeah, that's not a great thing—it at least buys us some momentum, and momentum is important in the decluttering process.

Now, though, it's time for me to start engaging the hard stuff. Most of the hard stuff made the first cut because it's tied in with memories. Maybe it's just me, but clutter tied with memories can be downright painful to let go and that can lead to paralysis in decision making. Because of this, it is critical that we stay in God's Word and keep His truth before us moment by moment!

Declutter paralysis is real. In order to stay on track or jar ourselves back into gear, we're going to spend this week asking some clarifying questions that, hopefully, will let God's Word correct our muddled (aka sinful) thinking. These questions will help us determine if we're actually living out what we say we believe. I know. Ouch! Remember, I'm not pointing fingers at you, I'm primarily writing to myself. So, let me rephrase, "These questions will help *me* determine if *I'm* actually living out what I say I believe." There. Better?

Asking Important Questions

How did I get all of this stuff? I've been asking myself that question for years, but I've noticed that the answers have changed over time. Sometimes I hang on to memories. Sometimes I hoard "assets." Sometimes I'm just not paying attention to what is going on around me because I'm busy with other things.

This week we're going to ask some questions and look at Scripture to help us navigate when we see paralysis on the horizon. We'll formulate questions that drive below the simple, "Should it stay or should it go?" There are so many more that we could use, but here are some clarifying questions that I've been asking myself:

- ***Where Is My Hope Set?***

(If I can't give something or get rid of it because I think it has too much value, what or who am I trusting?)

- ***Can This Bless Someone Else?***

(You may be surprised where this one ends up!)

- ***Does This Help Me Remember What God Wants Me To Remember?***

(Stones of remembrance . . . they're a thing!)

Where Is My Hope Set?

I enter the closet boldly. I will not keep what I do not wear. I am resolved to purge! I will send it away . . . And yet, what if I **do** *fit into that size within the next couple of months? Isn't that a bad use of assets? Or maybe I could sell them? . . . .*

Do my actions align with where I say my hope is set?

While there are so many places we could go to consider our heart towards perceived assets, this week we're going to start by looking at just two passages that spell out clearly a core reason many people hang onto things.

Scripture:

As we come to these two passages from Psalms and Proverbs, we see God inspiring the work of father and son. Most of Proverbs is attributed to Israel's King Solomon, the wealthiest and wisest man in the world in his day. His father, King David, wrote Psalm 20 and many other psalms as well.

READ Proverbs 18:10-11 and Psalm 20. Mark references to earthly things people put their trust in. Also mark every reference to the *Lord/God*.

Proverbs 18:10-11

10 The name of the Lord is a strong tower;
   The righteous runs into it and is safe.

11 A rich man's wealth is his strong city,
   And like a high wall in his own imagination.

Psalm 20

1 May the Lord answer you in the day of trouble!
   May the name of the God of Jacob set you securely on high!

2 May He send you help from the sanctuary
   And support you from Zion!

3 May He remember all your meal offerings
   And find your burnt offering acceptable! Selah.

4 May He grant you your heart's desire
   And fulfill all your counsel!

5 We will sing for joy over your victory,
   And in the name of our God we will set up our banners.
   May the Lord fulfill all your petitions.

6 Now I know that the Lord saves His anointed;
   He will answer him from His holy heaven
   With the saving strength of His right hand.

7 Some boast in chariots and some in horses,
   But we will boast in the name of the Lord, our God.

8 They have bowed down and fallen,
   But we have risen and stood upright.

9 Save, O Lord;
   May the King answer us in the day we call.

Reason through the Scriptures:

According to Proverbs 18:11, what does a rich man think his wealth provides him? Does it?

What is the problem with a rich man's view of his wealth? Is what he trusts real? Explain.

By contrast, where can people find true safety?

Okay, let's get to it. What "strong cities" and "high walls" are in your imagination? Regardless of the state of your bank account, are you ever tempted to think money is the answer to your problems? Why/why not? What kinds of real problems does this lead to?

Let's consider Psalm 20 now. What type of situation does David address in this psalm?

What does he pray for his hearers?

How does David's hope contrast with those he refers to in verse 7?

Living Content in a Material World

Lesson Five
Questions to Ask

77

What do you think horses and chariots represent? Not sure? Take a look at Deuteronomy 17:14-20.

According to both of these passages, where is true hope in troubling days?

Now, how can we apply this truth? Will anything in your closet give you true security? How can this truth affect your decisions about things in your home that you aren't currently using?

Scripture:

Before we move on, let's lean into the truth of true hope in one more passage. As we pick up in Hebrews 6, the author of Hebrews has been addressing the topic of falling away and encouraging his readers that he is "convinced of better things" concerning them and exhorting them regarding hope. Read all of Hebrews 6 in your Bible, then zero in on verses 16-20 here.

READ Hebrews 6:16-20 and mark every reference to *God* and to *hope*.

Hebrews 6:16-20

16 *For men swear by one greater* than themselves, *and with them an oath* given *as confirmation is an end of every dispute.*

17 *In the same way God, desiring even more to show to the heirs of the promise the unchangeableness of His purpose, interposed with an oath,*

18 *so that by two unchangeable things in which it is impossible for God to lie, we who have taken refuge would have strong encouragement to take hold of the hope set before us.*

> 19 This hope we have as an anchor of the soul, a hope *both sure and steadfast and one which enters within the veil,*
>
> 20 *where Jesus has entered as a forerunner for us, having become a high priest forever according to the order of Melchizedek.*

Reason through the Scriptures:

According to verse 18, what are we to "take hold of"?

What does this passage teach about hope?

How does this hope differ from varying forms of "hope" the world offers?

What makes this hope sure?

What did you learn about God in this passage? What does this have to do with your hope?

Is there anything in your closet that can anchor your soul?

Can I Bless Someone Else?

While I can resolve in my heart and mind that my hope is in Christ alone, questions still pop up as I purge material items from my house. At the top of my list: *Will I regret giving this away?* I have found some truths in Scripture to help me through this one!

So let's head to the book of Acts for some helpful exhortation remembering that the behavior of the church here is descriptive, not prescriptive. In other words, it describes what has happened in the past—and more specifically in Jerusalem—as opposed to prescribing or commanding what should happen in the future.

Scripture:

Let's look at these Acts passages one at a time. For Acts 4:32-37, I would encourage you to read all of chapters 4 and 5 to get more of the story on giving in the early church.

READ Acts 4:32-37 and mark references to *those who believed* including pronouns.

Acts 4:32-37

32 And the congregation of those who believed were of one heart and soul; and *not one* of them *claimed that anything belonging to him was his own, but all things were common property to them.*

33 And with great power the apostles were giving testimony to the resurrection of the Lord Jesus, and abundant grace was upon them all.

34 For there was not a needy person among them, for all who were owners of land or houses would sell them and bring the proceeds of the sales

35 and lay them at the apostles' feet, and they would be distributed to each as any had need.

36 Now Joseph, a Levite of Cyprian birth, who was also called Barnabas by the apostles (which translated means Son of Encouragement),

37 and who owned a tract of land, sold it and brought the money and laid it at the apostles' feet.

Lesson Five
Questions to Ask

Reason through the Scriptures:

What characterized the congregation's thinking and beliefs?

Have you ever experienced unity like this? If so, briefly describe it. Did your unity of heart affect your actions?

How did the early church's oneness of "heart and soul" affect their behavior?

What powered this thinking and behavior?

Compare what is happening here with what Jesus prayed for in John 17:22-23.

Why wasn't there a needy person among them?

Did everyone sell everything? Let's consider this by seeing if any Christians in Acts had houses. Consult the following verses and record what you find.

Acts 9:11

Acts 10:6

Acts 12:12

Acts 17:5

Acts 18:7

Given what you've noted in these cross-references, what do you think was happening?

What are ways today that your local church meets needs? What are ways you do?

Have you ever had someone meet a need *for* you? What effect did that have on you? Write it down and hold that thought!

Lesson Five
Questions to Ask

Bigger Barns

Scripture:

Before we leave Acts, let's take a look at Paul's words to the elders at the church in Ephesus as he left their region knowing he would not see them again.

READ Acts 20:31-38 and mark references to *Paul* including pronouns. As you begin, remember Paul is speaking.

Acts 20:31-38

31 "Therefore be on the alert, remembering that night and day for a period of three years I did not cease to admonish each one with tears.

32 "And now I commend you to God and to the word of His grace, which is able to build you up and to give you the inheritance among all those who are sanctified.

33 "I have coveted no one's silver or gold or clothes.

34 "You yourselves know that these hands ministered to my own needs and to the men who were with me.

35 "In everything I showed you that by working hard in this manner you must help the weak and remember the words of the Lord Jesus, that He Himself said, 'It is more blessed to give than to receive.'"

36 When he had said these things, he knelt down and prayed with them all.

37 And they began to weep aloud and embraced Paul, and repeatedly kissed him,

38 grieving especially over the word which he had spoken, that they would not see his face again. And they were accompanying him to the ship.

Reason through the Scriptures:

What did you learn about Paul in these verses? Look back where you marked references to him and make a simple list.

What does he specifically say he has *not* done?

Living Content in a Material World

Lesson Five
Questions to Ask

If someone made a similar statement today, what three things would make the list of typically coveted items?

Who does Paul say took care of his needs and the needs of those who were with him? Check out Acts 18:1-3 as you answer for more specifics.

What example had Paul set according to verse 35? Why was this important?

According to Paul, what did Jesus say about giving and receiving?

When you hesitate to give something away that you don't actually use or need, do you fear that it is too dangerous (i.e. "I might need it later . . . ") or too costly (i.e. "I spent too much on it . . . " or "I could sell it for something . . . ") to let go of? Or is it some other reason? Explain.

Okay, now remember I told you to hold that thought earlier about how amazing it was to have someone meet your need by giving you something? What does Jesus say is *even* better, more blessed, than receiving? How can this truth help you over the speed bump of hesitation?

Does this Help Me Remember What God Wants Me to Remember?

Throughout the Bible God tells His people to remember. Scripture records countless visual and physical reminders that God provides to help His people in this arena from the rainbow, to circumcision (ouch!), to tassels on clothing, to words on tablets, to stones piled up at Gilgal, just to name a few.

God wants His people to remember His covenant, His character, and His provision. Unfortunately, we often remember that which doesn't truly matter much like the wandering Israelites who rather than recalling God's strong arm in setting them free from bondage, longed for the onions they left behind in Egypt.

Scripture:

One of the most beautiful accounts we have in Scripture of God telling His people to remember is recorded in Joshua 4:1-7. As we come to the passage, the children of Israel have just crossed through the Jordan River—which had been at flood stage—to enter the Promised Land. Similar to the Red Sea crossing 40 years earlier in its miraculous nature, yet distinct in the specifics, the Jordan River crossing showed God's power and work in the nation's life to a new generation.

READ Joshua 4:1-7 and mark every reference to the *twelve stones*.

1. Now when all the nation had finished crossing the Jordan, the LORD spoke to Joshua, saying,
2. "Take for yourselves twelve men from the people, one man from each tribe,
3. and command them, saying, 'Take up for yourselves twelve stones from here out of the middle of the Jordan, from the place where the priests' feet are standing firm, and carry them over with you and lay them down in the lodging place where you will lodge tonight.' "

4 So Joshua called the twelve men whom he had appointed from the sons of Israel, one man from each tribe;

5 and Joshua said to them, "Cross again to the ark of the LORD your God into the middle of the Jordan, and each of you take up a stone on his shoulder, according to the number of the tribes of the sons of Israel.

6 "Let this be a sign among you, so that when your children ask later, saying, 'What do these stones mean to you?'

7 then you shall say to them, 'Because the waters of the Jordan were cut off before the ark of the covenant of the LORD; when it crossed the Jordan, the waters of the Jordan were cut off.' So these stones shall become a memorial to the sons of Israel forever."

Continue reading through the remainder of the chapter for additional context if you have time.

Reason through the Scriptures:

When does the LORD speak to Joshua? What does He tell Joshua to do?

What is significant about the stones? What are they to do with them?

According to verse 6, what are they to serve as? What should they cause the children to ask?

What message does the LORD want them to pass down through their generations?

Lesson Five
Questions to Ask

Do you have any memorials or stones of remembrance in your family, items with a story that remind you of the faithfulness of God? Explain.

As you have been decluttering, have you uncovered items that remind you of God's faithfulness in a particular season? If so, take a few moments to write down the memory and attach it to items that can be passed down to help the next generation remember the goodness and faithfulness of God.

Reviewing the Progress

Week 1—Kitchen / Dining

Week 2—Living / Family Room

Week 3—Master Bedroom

Week 4—Other Bedrooms

What we (again, not the royal "we," but the "we" of you in submission to God) accomplished:

What remains:

What was tougher than I thought and the truth I used to overcome it:

Week 5—Office / Other — YOU ARE HERE

Week 6—Bathrooms / Laundry

Remember to ask (and answer!!) these questions this week if you find yourself locking up:

- *Where is my hope set?*

- *Can this item bless someone else?*

- *Does this help me remember what God wants me to remember?*

One more thing, you're close to falling in a pit if you find yourself saying . . .

"But we could . . ." or *"But what if we . . ."*

Friends, pretty much anything that starts with "But" after you've decided to divest yourself of one of your faux "Preciouses" is going to be a problem.

In addition to books, here's another problem area for me! I've already brought a whole duffle bag to my folks' house to use as "swim caps"! LOL

Lesson Five
Questions to Ask

Bigger Barns

Work through your home office or other room of your choice this week continuing to use your audio Bible to go wide in God's Word in at least 15-minute increments. If you've finished the Gospels, I encourage you to continue through the remainder of the New Testament. Remember to jot down something you want to remember each day. Again, this is just to help you stay engaged.

Day 1

Day 2

Day 3

Day 4

Day 5

Day 6

Day 7

ASK THE QUESTIONS!

LESSON SIX

For What Purpose?

GOD HAS CALLED YOU TO HIS MISSION! ARE YOU ON IT?

When we started our journey six weeks ago, we encountered the story of a man whose goal was to take his ease, eat, drink, and be merry by his own hand through his own power. Then he died and his goal died with him. His stored up treasures on earth, remained on earth. He had not sent them ahead.

Jesus calls His people to more! He calls His people to purpose, to mission, to Himself. Knowing our God-given purpose gives us a tangible way to help assess what to keep and what to throw.

When downsizing her life into a few suitcases and a storage unit so she could move overseas to bring the Gospel to a closed country, my friend Katherine asked the question "For what purpose?"

Think about it. That question works on so many levels . . .

- *For what purpose am I here?*
- *For what purpose should I keep this?*
- *For what purpose should I give this?*

Lesson Six
For What Purpose?

Simply asking "For what purpose?" will surface the answers to other underlying questions. Questions like . . .

- *What matters most?*
- *How will keeping, giving, or throwing affect me and others from a Kingdom perspective?*
- *Will this feed my greed or my generosity?*
- *Who do I look like more when I do this—my earthly family of birth or my adoptive heavenly Father?*
- *Does this set my eyes on the Kingdom and the city to come or does it anchor me to "the good life" or the sorrows here?*
- *Does this feed fear or encourage faith?*

As we jump into our final week of study, let's consider what our purpose should be according to Jesus. Who and what should we ultimately *love* and *not love*?

Does My Stuff Align With My Mission?

When a lawyer asks Jesus about the greatest commandment—the most important thing for God's followers to do—Jesus responds by quoting from both Deuteronomy and Leviticus. Let's look at His answer, as well as the sources He quotes before we start asking questions.

Scripture:

READ Matthew 22:34-40 and mark references to *love*.

Matthew 22:34-40

34 But when the Pharisees heard that Jesus had silenced the Sadducees, they gathered themselves together.

35 One of them, a lawyer, asked Him a question, testing Him,

36 "Teacher, which is the great commandment in the Law?"

37 And He said to him, " 'YOU SHALL LOVE THE LORD YOUR GOD WITH ALL YOUR HEART, AND WITH ALL YOUR SOUL, AND WITH ALL YOUR MIND.'

38 "This is the great and foremost commandment.

39 "The second is like it, 'YOU SHALL LOVE YOUR NEIGHBOR AS YOURSELF.'

40 "On these two commandments depend the whole Law and the Prophets."

READ Deuteronomy 6:4-13 and circle all of the commands. Note that Moses delivers these words from God to the people of Israel when they are in the land of Moab just prior to entering the Promised Land.

Deuteronomy 6:4-13

4 "Hear, O Israel! The LORD is our God, the LORD is one!

5 "You shall love the LORD your God with all your heart and with all your soul and with all your might.

6 "These words, which I am commanding you today, shall be on your heart.

7 "You shall teach them diligently to your sons and shall talk of them when you sit in your house and when you walk by the way and when you lie down and when you rise up.

8 "You shall bind them as a sign on your hand and they shall be as frontals on your forehead.

9 "You shall write them on the doorposts of your house and on your gates.

10 "Then it shall come about when the LORD your God brings you into the land which He swore to your fathers, Abraham, Isaac and Jacob, to give you, great and splendid cities which you did not build,

11 and houses full of all good things which you did not fill, and hewn cisterns which you did not dig, vineyards and olive trees which you did not plant, and you eat and are satisfied,

12 then watch yourself, that you do not forget the LORD who brought you from the land of Egypt, out of the house of slavery.

13 "You shall fear only the LORD your God; and you shall worship Him and swear by His name.

For more context read all of Deuteronomy 6.

READ Leviticus 19:15-18 and mark references to *your neighbor*.

Leviticus 19:15-18

15 'You shall do no injustice in judgment; you shall not be partial to the poor nor defer to the great, but you are to judge your neighbor fairly.

16 'You shall not go about as a slanderer among your people, and you are not to act against the life of your neighbor; I am the LORD.

17 'You shall not hate your fellow countryman in your heart; you may surely reprove your neighbor, but shall not incur sin because of him.

18 'You shall not take vengeance, nor bear any grudge against the sons of your people, but you shall love your neighbor as yourself; I am the LORD.

Reason through the Scriptures:

Questions on Matthew

Who initiates the conversation in Matthew 22:34-40? What do we know about him?

What question does he ask Jesus? Why does he ask?

How does Jesus respond? Does He answer the exact question that was asked Him? Explain.

Where does Jesus answer from in verse 37 and what does He say?

Questions on Deuteronomy

According to Deuteronomy 1:1-4 what is the setting of this book? Where are the Israelites when they hear these words? Where have they been and where are they heading?

Living Content in a Material World

For What Purpose?

What does God command the people to do in Deuteronomy 6:4-13?

What are they specifically to do with regard to their children?

What are they supposed to do with these commands as they pertain to what they wear and where they live?

What does God say He is going to give the Israelites in verse 11?

What condition will this bring about according to verse 11? Is this bad or wrong? Explain.

How do you think being well fed and satisfied affects Christians today? Do you think we pay attention to this? Explain.

Lesson Six
For What Purpose?

Bigger Barns

According to verse 12, what danger will come with the new condition? If you know the biblical storyline, how does this play out in Israel's history?

What causes people today to forget or ignore God? When are you tempted to forget or ignore God? How does this typically play out in your life?

Before we move on to the Leviticus cross-reference, I have to tell you a little story. Those who know my daughter, Katie, know that she is a party waiting to happen. While I'm happy to see people occasionally and my dog regularly, Katie thrives on "the people" (say it with inflection!). For the past four years of college, "the people" have been mainly other believers from Wheaton College home with us for Thanksgiving, floor retreats, Easter . . . you name it. Our house is normal to them because they are accustomed to Christian people "writing on their doorposts." Prior to bringing Wheaton College home with her, however, Katie brought Warren High School home for Friendsgiving and other events during high school. I'll never forget her high school friends looking around the house and commenting that we had so many "words on our walls." ... and there are more, a lot more!

It caught me off-guard because we habituate to what is around us all the time, but as I surveyed the room we were in, it was true, there were a lot of words on the walls!

"Writing on our doorposts," so to speak, is one physical way we remember in this household.

How do you actively remember the LORD? Think of something simple you can share that might encourage others who are studying with you.

What have you learned about remembering the LORD from others?

We've covered this before, but let's consider it again: Does your "stuff"—physical or mental—point you to God or distract you from Him? If you need a change, where will you start?

Questions on Leviticus

Now let's consider Leviticus 19:15-18. What is the main topic of these verses?

Lesson Six
For What Purpose?

Bigger Barns

Given the context of Jesus' quotation from Leviticus, how much do you think concern for our neighbor should factor into our general life mission? How does your life line up with Jesus' teaching on this? If you're wondering, "Who is my neighbor?" read Luke 10:25-37.

How do you think the primacy of the command to love God and love neighbor will impact a disciple's view of material possessions?

How does your attitude toward material possessions affect your ability to love your neighbors? Is it positive, negative, or somewhere in between? Explain.

Do you share with an open hand? Do you allow others who want to let you use their abundance minister to you? How well do you both give and receive? Explain.

Sharing back and forth can cause us to connect when we wouldn't otherwise make the time.

As I think about my things while I'm writing, I'm realizing how much I *love* my printer. I have the stable, always-reliable printer in the neighborhood. My next door neighbors have a printer, but it's cranky. Because of this, my printer serves my mission of writing AND it builds bridges with my neighbors.

My neighbors do not need to buy a printer and I don't need to buy certain lawn tools. Borrowing a hoe for an afternoon is a good excuse to go chat with my neighbor!

What Not to Love . . .

Jesus is clear that we are to love God and love others, but His Word is also clear about what true disciples do NOT love. We find this clear word in 1 John 2.

Scripture:

If there were a straight path for you to find this on your own, I would prompt you in that direction. However, since it is a bit of a circuitous route, I will simply tell you that the Greek root word translated "lust" (*epithumia*) in 1 John 2 is the same that appears in the *LXX* (aka the *Septuagint,* the Greek translation of the Old Testament) and is translated as "covet."

READ 1 John 2:15-17 and mark references to *love*, to *lust/s,* and to *the world*.

> *1 John 2:15-17*
>
> 15 Do not love the world nor the things in the world. If anyone loves the world, the love of the Father is not in him.
>
> 16 For all that is in the world, the lust of the flesh and the lust of the eyes and the boastful pride of life, is not from the Father, but is from the world.
>
> 17 The world is passing away, and also its lusts; but the one who does the will of God lives forever.

There's more for you in the full chapter!

Reason through the Scriptures:

What does John say his readers should not love? Why?

What does John say about *the world* in these verses? What characterizes it? How long will it last?

Lesson Six
For What Purpose?

Bigger Barns

Do you see a correlation between "all that is in the world" and "all that is in your house"? If you were to make a Venn diagram—you know, those overlapping circles—how much of "all that is in the world" and "all that is in your house" overlap?

Is there any improper material in your house that just needs to go, things that could be associated with the "lust of the flesh"? (Perhaps books you wouldn't want your kids to pick up or movies that would make your Grandma blush.) Don't write it down, just throw it out.

Are there things in your house that you could not afford, but just "had to have," items that made their way into your house because of the "lust of the eyes"? If yes, jot them down.

Are you holding on to items that feed your ego and display "the boastful pride of life"? Again, write them down.

What do your possessions say about who or what you love? Do you like what they are saying? (By now, you *may be liking* what they are saying! This isn't necessarily a downer question!)

Living Content in a Material World

Lesson Six
For What Purpose?

According to these verses, what is ephemeral and what endures? How can this help clarify decision making?

How does this compare with John 3:16 where Jesus says that "God so loved the world"? How are they both true?

Run Light!

Hebrews 12 sits in the shadow of the more flashy and famous Hebrews 11. Eleven, often dubbed the "Hall of Faith," recounts men and women of faith throughout the ages of biblical history. Hebrews 12 calls readers to a life of faith like those who ran the race in Hebrews 11. Read both chapters together before diving in here..

Scripture:

READ Hebrews 12:1-13 and mark the verbs in verses 1-3 and the word *discipline* throughout the passage.

1 *Therefore, since we have so great a cloud of witnesses surrounding us, let us also lay aside every encumbrance and the sin which so easily entangles us, and let us run with endurance the race that is set before us,*

2 *fixing our eyes on Jesus, the author and perfecter of faith, who for the joy set before Him endured the cross, despising the shame, and has sat down at the right hand of the throne of God.*

3 *For consider Him who has endured such hostility by sinners against Himself, so that you will not grow weary and lose heart.*

4 *You have not yet resisted to the point of shedding blood in your striving against sin;*

5 and you have forgotten the exhortation which is addressed to you as sons, "MY SON, DO NOT REGARD LIGHTLY THE DISCIPLINE OF THE LORD, NOR FAINT WHEN YOU ARE REPROVED BY HIM;

6 FOR THOSE WHOM THE LORD LOVES HE DISCIPLINES, AND HE SCOURGES EVERY SON WHOM HE RECEIVES."

7 It is for discipline that you endure; God deals with you as with sons; for what son is there whom his father does not discipline?

8 But if you are without discipline, of which all have become partakers, then you are illegitimate children and not sons.

9 Furthermore, we had earthly fathers to discipline us, and we respected them; shall we not much rather be subject to the Father of spirits, and live?

10 For they disciplined us for a short time as seemed best to them, but He disciplines us for our good, so that we may share His holiness.

11 All discipline for the moment seems not to be joyful, but sorrowful; yet to those who have been trained by it, afterwards it yields the peaceful fruit of righteousness.

12 Therefore, strengthen the hands that are weak and the knees that are feeble,

13 and make straight paths for your feet, so that the limb which is lame may not be put out of joint, but rather be healed.

Reason through the Scriptures:

According to the author of Hebrews, what are we to lay aside and why?

What do encumbrances and sins have in common?

Where may they differ?

Do you think an encumbrance could ever be a good thing in some contexts, but something that weighs down in others? Explain.

Generally speaking, what is the race that is set before us? (You may want to compare with Hebrews 11.)

As we run, where are our eyes to be fixed? What are we to consider and to what purpose?

I was tempted to end our study with "throw off the encumbrances," but I'm struck by verses 4-13 and the key word *paideia* (translated here as "discipline"). So before we conclude let's consider this word more closely.

Look back at everywhere you've marked the word *discipline*. Now, make a simple list of everything you learned about it in this passage.

Lesson Six
For What Purpose?

Let's see how the noun *paideia* (the same form that we saw in Hebrews), as well as the verb *paideuo* are used in some other New Testament passages.

    Acts 7:22

    Acts 22:3

    Ephesians 6:4

    2 Timothy 2:25

    2 Timothy 3:16

    Titus 2:12

    Revelation 3:19

You can use your study tools to find more about this Greek word.

Summarize below what you've learned about *paideia*.

As we've considered the problem of clutter—physical and otherwise—has the Spirit been convicting you of sin in this regard or have you been encouraged that your life is in balance? Explain.

If moments of this class have been in some way "sorrowful," what hope does Hebrews 12:11 offer?

Lesson Six

For What Purpose?

What is God bringing about in us when He deals with sin in our lives?

What does Hebrews liken this to in verses 12-13?

How can we best submit to this work in our lives?

How can we support others who are going through this?

Paul's Secret!

Much or little, it didn't matter to Paul. He knew the secret to contentment and he shares it with the Philippians—and us—as he closes his letter to the church at Philippi. Read Philippians 4 before breaking down the verses below.

Scripture:

READ Philippians 4:10-14 and mark references to *Paul* and to the *Lord*.

> 10 But I rejoiced in the Lord greatly, that now at last you have revived your concern for me; indeed, you were concerned before, but you lacked opportunity.

11 Not that I speak from want, for I have learned to be content in whatever circumstances I am.

12 I know how to get along with humble means, and I also know how to live in prosperity; in any and every circumstance I have learned the secret of being filled and going hungry, both of having abundance and suffering need.

13 I can do all things through Him who strengthens me.

14 Nevertheless, you have done well to share with me *in my affliction.*

Reason through the Scriptures:

Do circumstances ruffle Paul? Explain.

What does he say he has learned? What is the secret that he knows?

Where does his strength come from?

Have you learned Paul's secret?

Are you able to be content and get along with humble means? What challenges have you faced in this?

Do you know how to be content and live in prosperity? What challenges has this posed for you?

How has/can the Lord strengthen in both circumstances?

Reviewing the Progress

Week 1—Kitchen / Dining

Week 2—Living / Family Room

Week 3—Master Bedroom

Week 4—Other Bedrooms

Week 5—Office / Other

What we (again, not the royal "we," but the "we" of you in submission to God) accomplished:

Lesson Six
For What Purpose?

What remains:

What I uncovered that brought me joy this week:

Week 6—Bathrooms / Laundry — YOU ARE HERE

Remember to ask (and answer!!) these questions this week and as you go forward if you find yourself locking up:

- *Does this help me love God better or turn my eyes from Him?*

- *Can I use this to show love to my neighbors? OR Will this cause me to become "The Jones"?*

- *Does this propel me on or detract me from my mission? Does it make what I'm called to do easier and more effective? OR Does this take time, energy, attention, and money away from what God has for me to do and be?*

Living Content in a Material World

Lesson Six
For What Purpose?

WIDE

Keep listening as you continue to sort and purge. Listening through the New Testament will take about 20 hours and is a great way to redeem the time and focus your mind on the things of the Kingdom as you wade through the stuff of the earth! You may regret things you have bought and squirreled away and saved, but you will never regret time invested in God's Word!

Remember to jot down something you want to remember each day. Again, this is just to help you stay engaged.

Day 1

Day 2

Day 3

Day 4

Day 5

Day 6

Day 7

> "After these things the word of the LORD came to Abram in a vision, saying,
> "Do not be afraid, Abram. I am your shield, your exceedingly great reward."
> —Genesis 15:1 (NKJV)

HE IS THE SHIELD, HE IS THE REWARD!

Wrapping Up

In Philippians 4:11-12 Paul tells the Philippians that he has "learned" how to be content. It encourages me to know that Paul had to learn contentment because if he learned it, we can learn it, too. Don't you love the hope in that?! Be encouraged!

As we continue pursuing God through His Word and thinking biblically about our physical possessions, my hope is that we will learn to be content in whatever circumstances we find ourselves, whether it is with little or much by the world's standards.

My prayer for you and me is that we will evaluate all of our stuff in light of the Kingdom of God and that we will look at everything in our lives through the lens of our mission as Christ's ambassadors in this world always asking the question: *Does this help propel me on mission or does this in some way oppose it?*

Let us live as citizens of another country, always remembering that even the finest of earthly treasures has a shelf-life and eventually succumbs to moths, rust, mice, and their ilk. Only what is sent ahead, only treasures stored up in heaven will last.

I've come a long way since I started this journey. I'm guessing you have, too. While we still have room to grow—at least I do—be encouraged, my friend, by the progress that you've made and know that God is not finished with you yet!

So, until we meet again, may God bless you and keep you and cause His face to shine upon you and give you peace.

Contentedly and unencumbered,

Pam

Lesson Five
Questions to Ask